Knowledge Graphs

Dieter Fensel • Umutcan Şimşek • Kevin Angele •
Elwin Huaman • Elias Kärle •
Oleksandra Panasiuk • Ioan Toma •
Jürgen Umbrich • Alexander Wahler

Knowledge Graphs

Methodology, Tools and Selected Use Cases

 Springer

Dieter Fensel
Semantic Technology Institute Innsbruck,
Department of Computer Science
University of Innsbruck
Innsbruck, Tirol, Austria

Kevin Angele
Semantic Technology Institute Innsbruck,
Department of Computer Science,
University of Innsbruck,
Innsbruck, Tirol, Austria

Onlim GmbH
Telfs, Tirol, Austria

Elias Kärle
Semantic Technology Institute Innsbruck,
Department of Computer Science
University of Innsbruck
Innsbruck, Tirol, Austria

Ioan Toma
Onlim GmbH
Telfs, Tirol, Austria

Alexander Wahler
Onlim GmbH
Telfs, Tirol, Austria

Umutcan Şimşek
Semantic Technology Institute Innsbruck,
Department of Computer Science
University of Innsbruck
Innsbruck, Tirol, Austria

Elwin Huaman
Semantic Technology Institute Innsbruck,
Department of Computer Science
University of Innsbruck
Innsbruck, Tirol, Austria

Oleksandra Panasiuk
Semantic Technology Institute Innsbruck,
Department of Computer Science
University of Innsbruck
Innsbruck, Tirol, Austria

Jürgen Umbrich
Onlim GmbH
Telfs, Tirol, Austria

ISBN 978-3-030-37438-9   ISBN 978-3-030-37439-6   (eBook)
https://doi.org/10.1007/978-3-030-37439-6

This Springer imprint is published by the registered company Springer Nature Switzerland AG.
The registered company address is: Gewerbestrasse 11, 6330 Cham, Switzerland

Foreword

In 2005, Manuel Sahli became an active contributor to Wikipedia. He was particularly interested in his hometown, the beautiful Swiss city of Winterthur. Over the years, he edited and meticulously maintained the article on Winterthur. One of the sections he worked on was the list of sister cities.

Around the same time, a contributor added Winterthur to the list of sister cities on the article on Ontario, California, a city about an hour east of Los Angeles. Even though sister cities are supposed to be reciprocal, the information never made it to the article on Winterthur.

Manuel, although interested in all things Winterthur, did not learn about this addition for almost a decade.

2012 saw the launch of Wikidata, a sister project of Wikipedia. It was a Knowledge Graph that anyone could edit and use. As time went by, a contributor added the list of sister cities of Ontario to Wikidata, using the Ontario article on Wikipedia.

Manuel Sahli had since been elected to the cantonal parliament of Winterthur. Using Wikidata, he wanted to make a map of Winterthur's sister cities and Wikidata has a powerful query interface that allows creating ad hoc visualizations of query results over its Knowledge Graph. To Manuel's big surprise, the map contained one place he was not familiar with yet: Ontario.

At first, Manuel thought that this was an act of vandalism that has remained undiscovered for a while, but the fact came with a source: the official government website of Ontario. When he went to that site, there he found Winterthur! As a member of the cantonal parliament, he asked the Winterthur city administration and archives if they knew anything about that claim. Both denied.

Manuel wrote an official letter to the city of Ontario to clarify the situation, and lo and behold, they delivered documents, signed by both sides, establishing the sister city relation in 1982. Given these documents and the precise dates, the Winterthur city archives were now able to find the relevant documents. Thanks to Wikidata, Winterthur discovered its long lost fifth sister city, and the two cities have since rekindled their relationship.

No one was trying to hide that fact from Manuel or the world. The city archives had the documents (but could not find them at first), Wikipedia was publishing the fact for almost a decade, and it was on the official Ontario website, and yet Manuel, although deeply invested in his hometown and Wikipedia, did not learn about it. It was only when it was added to a Knowledge Graph, one that Manuel had access to and knew how to query, that the fact was surfaced.

It is far too easy to bury knowledge in documents and heaps of natural language and very hard to surface it at the right time. A Knowledge Graph makes facts easier to index, process, and find.

However, that is only half the story. The other half is that it was sheer luck that Manuel was not only interested enough to discover this fact but also capable of querying Wikidata using the SPARQL query language. Most people do not know how to do that.

We are witnessing a paradigm shift in how we use computers, as momentous as the introduction of time-sharing systems, graphical user interfaces, the web, and smartphones before: the nascent ability to interact with computers through natural language. Conversational interfaces have been around for a long time just as any novel technology has been preceded by various adoptions in niche areas. However, so-called intelligent assistants are quickly spreading and evolving, and more and more devices, from wristwatches to cars, from televisions to earbuds, are being equipped with the capability to listen to your commands and questions and to answer them.

The number of people who will gain access to knowledge through intelligent assistants for their daily tasks is growing remarkably fast. In order to find answers to burning questions, whether trivial or life-changing, we will not need the traditional computer in the office or school or library anymore. No one will need to learn how to use the newest smartphone features, how to use a mouse, or even how to read and type, thus widely opening the door to a much more inclusive world.

This new paradigm needs new ways to allow people to join the new data space, to give access to their data and their services to their prospective clients and consumers, and to allow people to discover and enjoy what they have to offer. In a world where more and more people do not use apps and websites to book a hotel room, rent a car, buy a flight ticket, order their lunch, and ask for information, we need to make sure to understand the users' intents and offer our data and services in ways that allow their integration and composition. This is not a vision of a future to come but the world we already built. Tens of thousands of capabilities and services are already integrated into the Google Assistant, Apple Siri, Amazon Alexa, the open source Mycroft, Microsoft Cortana, Samsung Bixby, and others.

Bringing together the natural language technology required to understand users' queries and the power of structuring facts in large Knowledge Graphs will allow us to bring knowledge to the end user when they need it. People will become empowered to explore and ask about the world, to follow their curiosity, to learn. Businesses will be able to expand the reach of their services and products to many new customers.

This book offers a hands-on overview of the architecture and the steps to join the world of intelligent assistants. It guides us through building, growing, and maintaining our Knowledge Graph. It discusses how Knowledge Graphs represent the facts that are important in your organization and how to make them available to other providers.

Dieter Fensel was one of the people who have very early recognized the potential of semantic technologies and the need to allow for the composition of services into novel interfaces. He and his research groups were leading the field in the semantic description of services, in linked data applications, and Ontology engineering and learning methods and tools. This book by him and the researchers of his team is distilling the experience of many years.

Enjoy going through the book! It will help you to better understand the novel field of Knowledge Graphs and how to use them. It will allow you and your organization to move to a world where the knowledge you already have in your archives and systems does not remain so stubbornly hidden and where you and your customers both will be enabled to work with the knowledge you already have, so that we can empower users, discover new sources of revenue, and never lose a sister city again.

San Francisco, CA, USA   Denny Vrandečić
June 2019

Preface

Smart speakers such as Alexa and Google Home introduced Artificial Intelligence (AI) in millions soon billions of households, making AI an everyday experience. We can now look for information, order products, and services without leaving the house or touching a computer. We just talk to a box and this thing will conveniently perform the desired tasks for us. These new communication channels define a new challenge for successful e-marketing and e-commerce. Just running a traditional website with many colorful pictures is no longer state of the art. Even the web is currently reinventing itself by applying schema.org. Data, content, and services become semantically annotated, allowing software agents, so-called bots, to search through the web understanding its content. The times where humans were browsing through large number of websites and manually extracting and interpreting their information are passing by. The users nowadays consult their personal bot to find, aggregate, and personalize information and to reserve, book, or buy products and services. In consequence, it becomes increasingly important for providers of information, products, and services to be highly hearable and visible in these new online channels to ensure their future economic sustainability. In this book, we discuss methods and tools helping to achieve these visibility goals. The core is the development and application of machine-processable (semantic) annotations of content, data, and services as well as their aggregation in large Knowledge Graphs. Only this enables bots to not only understand a question but being able to answer a question in a knowledgeable way.

These Knowledge Graphs, especially when based on schema.org, play an increasingly important role in Internet-based information search. They become a significant key technology for successful e-commerce and e-marketing and their influence on the value distribution in economic sectors that interact with their customers online. It is yet another approach for scalable data integration on a large scale and most likely it will not be the last approach tackling this very hard problem. However, it is also the first time that we approach this problem on a worldwide scale. In this book, we describe methods and tools that empower information providers to build and maintain such a Knowledge Graph. In particular, the following aspects will be introduced:

- Methods and tools for manual, semi-automatic, and automatic construction and validation plus verification of semantic annotations and their integration into Knowledge Graphs.
- Methods and tools for the implementation of Knowledge Graphs.
- Lifecycle-based approaches for semi-automatic and automatic curation of such graphs. This includes approaches for assessment, error correction, and enrichment of knowledge with other static and dynamic resources.

Knowledge is half the way. It must be made applicable as potential answers for questions and as guidance for a dialog.

- e-marketing: with reasoning methods and tools, we can derive dialog-based bots for specific tasks and domains from a Knowledge Graph.
- e-commerce: based on the semantic descriptions of services and products, a goal-oriented dialog can be designed improving the process of reserving, renting, booking, or buying goods and services.

To illustrate the practical usage of these approaches, we discuss several pilots with a focus on e-tourism domain. Tourism is one of the largest verticals worldwide with significant growth potential. Also, it is one of the verticals where Europe may have a future, and the distribution of value critically depends on proper competence in e-marketing and e-commerce. Potential customers are distributed worldwide, and service providers are fragmented, mostly small business units (e.g., tens of thousands of small family hotels in Tyrol). In general, we focus on the following aspects:

- Integration of content, data, and service descriptions from open, proprietary, heterogeneous, and distributed sources.
- Efficient and effective maintenance of context of data (e.g., provenance, geographical and temporal validity).
- Using Knowledge Graphs for guiding dialogs.
- Integration of static and dynamic sources.
- Integration of Semantic Web services to facilitate actions and automatic service invocation.

The structure of this book follows these arguments. Chapter 1 provides a definition for Knowledge Graphs. We do not aim for mathematical precision but rather try to cover the various approaches regarding their impact. Chapter 2 details how Knowledge Graphs are built, implemented, maintained, and deployed. Chapter 3 introduces relevant application layers that can be built with such Knowledge Graphs. We explain how inference can be used to define views on such a graph, making it a useful resource for open and service-oriented dialog systems. The proof of the pudding is in the eating. Chapter 4 elaborates application of Knowledge Graph technologies for e-tourism and use cases and pilots for other verticals. Chapter 5 provides a summary and sketches directions for future work. In Appendix A we introduce an abstract syntax and semantics for our domain specifications that are used to adapt schema.org to specific domains and tasks.

Innsbruck, Austria	Dieter Fensel
Innsbruck, Austria	Umutcan Şimşek
Innsbruck, Austria	Kevin Angele
Innsbruck, Austria	Elwin Huaman
Innsbruck, Austria	Elias Kärle
Innsbruck, Austria	Oleksandra Panasiuk
Telfs, Austria	Ioan Toma
Telfs, Austria	Jürgen Umbrich
Telfs, Austria	Alexander Wahler

Acknowledgment

We would like to thank Andreas Harth and Aidan Hogan for the very fruitful and helpful discussions and reviews of the book. Also, we would like to thank all participants of the MindLab project as the book summarizes the essence of their work.[1] Additionally, the very fruitful discussions we had with the participants of the 2019 STI Summit on Knowledge Graphs (especially with Mark Musen, Juan Sequeda, Rudi Studer, and Sung-Kook Han) helped significantly in sharping our conclusions.[2] Finally, we would like to thank Andreas Lackner for acting as a pathfinder for us to find through the labyrinth of (Tyrolean) e-tourism.

---

[1] https://mindlab.ai/

[2] https://www.sti2.org/events/2019-sti2-semantic-summit

Contents

Chapter 1
Introduction: What Is a Knowledge Graph?

Knowledge graphs are critical to many enterprises today:
They provide the structured data and factual knowledge that
drive many products and make them more intelligent and
magical. (Noy et al. 2019)

Abstract Since its inception by Google, Knowledge Graph has become a term that is recently ubiquitously used yet does not have a well-established definition. This section attempts to derive a definition for Knowledge Graphs by compiling existing definitions made in the literature and considering the distinctive characteristics of previous efforts for tackling the data integration challenge we are facing today. Our attempt to make a conceptual definition is complemented with an empirical survey of existing Knowledge Graphs. This section lays the foundation for the remainder of the book, as it provides a common understanding on certain concepts and motivation to build Knowledge Graphs in the first place.

1.1 Introduction

Smart speakers such as Alexa and Google Home introduced AI-based (AI) communication means in millions soon billions of households. Even the web is currently reinventing itself by applying schema.org[1] (Guha et al. 2016). Data, content, and services become semantically annotated, allowing a software agent, so-called bots,[2] to search through the web understanding its content. Therefore, it becomes increasingly important for information, service, and product providers to be highly hearable and visible in these new online channels to ensure their future economic maturity.

---

[1]https://www.schema.org/

[2]https://en.wikipedia.org/wiki/Internet_bot

© Springer Nature Switzerland AG 2020
D. Fensel et al., *Knowledge Graphs*, https://doi.org/10.1007/978-3-030-37439-6_1

The development of such automatic methods for speech recognition is an important prerequisite for the development of automated dialog systems.[3] Their breakthrough in automatic language understanding is based on Big Data[4] and machine learning (Goodfellow et al. 2016). However, for answering a query or for running a goal-oriented dialog, more is needed. For giving a meaningful answer, an agent needs knowledge. Therefore, Google started in 2012 to develop a so-called Knowledge Graph,[5] which should contain significant aspects of human knowledge found semantically annotated on the web or in other data sources. Meanwhile a kind of hype has arisen around this technology.[6] In consequence, it becomes necessary to better understand what Knowledge Graphs are about. We approach this question complementarily. First, we try to give a conceptual answer by analyzing the underlying principles of a Knowledge Graph. Second, we provide an empirical survey on existing Knowledge Graphs.

1.2   A Conceptual Definition of Knowledge Graphs

Size matters (unknown author, most likely male)

Ehrlinger and Wöß (2016) provides a very useful and concise survey on potential definitions of Knowledge Graphs illustrating their variations. They also add a new definition which is centered on using Ontologies and reasoners deriving new knowledge. From our point of view, this definition is too exclusive and too much focused on specific methods. Let us start with a few thoughts on potential *definitions* of a Knowledge Graph. Hermeneutically, we could first distinguish the two terms constituting this concept since we have two quite different beasts.

A "*graph* is a structure amounting to a set of objects in which some pairs of the objects are in some sense related".[7] Strictly spoken we need to slightly extend this definition to multi-sets since the same object can syntactically and semantically appear several times in our graph. Some normalization can get rid of this issue, but this already implies certain specific processing techniques. This simple definition can be extended in various directions and we end up with an entire zoo of graph types: simple graphs, undirected versus directed graphs, oriented graphs, mixed graphs, multigraphs, Quiver, weighted graphs, half-edges and loose-edges graphs,

---

[3]https://en.wikipedia.org/wiki/Dialogue_system

[4]https://en.wikipedia.org/wiki/Big_data

[5]A. Singhal: Introducing the Knowledge Graph, things, not strings. Blog post at http://googleblog.blogspot.co.uk/2012/05/introducing-knowledge-graph-things-not.html, 2012.

[6]Just to mention a few books (Chen et al. 2016; Croitoru et al. 2018; d'Amato and Theobald 2018; Ehrig et al. 2015; Li et al. 2017; Pan et al. 2017a, b; Qi et al., 2020; Qi et al. 2013; Van Erp et al. 2017). See also Bonatti et al. (2019).

[7]https://en.wikipedia.org/wiki/Graph_(discrete_mathematics).

finite versus infinite graphs, and more.[8] This reminds on the situation in the information system field in the last century when "every" new PhD introduced a new variant for Petri-Nets[9]: labelled, colored, hierarchical, etc. Just quoting Wikipedia: "There are many more extensions to Petri nets, however, it is important to keep in mind, that as the complexity of the net increases in terms of extended properties, the harder it is to use standard tools to evaluate certain properties of the net. For this reason, it is a good idea to use the simplest net type possible for a given modelling task."[10] In the Semantic Web community, the consensus is to use RDF as representation formalism for representing a Knowledge Graph.[11] However, when looking precisely, it is often the case that RDF[12] is rather used syntactically than also epistemologically or semantically. For example, RDF provides only global property definitions and often one would like to use properties defined as attributes with specific ranges for a concept for which they are defined.[13] Similarly, RDF/OWL semantics that interprets range restriction as a means to infer new knowledge instead of using them to detect type errors is not necessarily the intended meaning of range definitions in schema.org.[14,15]

The concept of *knowledge* is a bit fluffier. Let us go back to what (Newell 1982) called the knowledge level. Based on the assumption that an agent follows the principle of rationality (later refined to the concept of *bounded rationality* (Simon 1957) including the costs for "optimal" decision-making), we subscribe knowledge to it perceiving the actions it takes to achieve certain goals. In this sense, knowledge is externally assigned to this agent by an observer. Internally the "knowledge" is coded at the symbol level.

> Beneath the knowledge level resides the symbol level. Whereas the knowledge level is *world* oriented, namely that it concerns the environment in which the agent operates, the symbol level is *system* oriented, in that it includes the mechanisms the agent has available to operate. The knowledge level *rationalizes* the agent's behavior, while the symbol level *mechanizes* the agent's behavior (Newell 1982).

---

[8]https://en.wikipedia.org/wiki/Graph_(discrete_mathematics). See Angles and Gutiérrez (2005) for a comprehensive survey on Graph and Models.

[9]http://www.scholarpedia.org/article/Petri_net. See also Reisig (2013).

[10]https://en.wikipedia.org/wiki/Petri_net

[11]See Angles and Gutiérrez (2008) for a survey on graph databases.

[12]https://www.w3.org/RDF/

[13]Hayes (1981) and Patel-Schneider (2014). Guha et al. (2016) already extend RDF by polymorphism, and the large number of sub-properties in schema.org tries to bypass this bottleneck of RDF. See also Patel-Schneider (2014).

[14]https://schema.org /

[15]A note for informed readers: Assume the class human and the property birthplace with a range city. If an RDF/OWL reasoner finds the statements *{birthPlace(*domain:*Human,range:City, human (*Hans*), birthPlace(Hans)* = *"Austria"}*, it infers that "Austria" is a city instead of identifying a range error. See also Sect. 2.4.1. See also De Bruijn et al. (2005), Patel-Schneider and Horrocks (2006).

We could similarly interpret the Knowledge Graph. An agent has/generates knowledge by interpreting a graph, i.e., relates its elements to so-called real-world objects and actions. Moreover, a graph is a specific encoding formalism. To refine it a bit more, we may want to put the graph at the *logical* or *epistemological level* rather than at the implementational level (Brachman 1979). At the *implementational level*, we have means such as graph-based databases.

On the one hand it is not straightforward to distinguish Knowledge Graphs from semantic nets,[16] a popular knowledge representation formalism in the 1960s and 1970s of the last century (Brachman 1990; Sowa 1992). On the other hand, the obvious difference is their actual size and therefore the potential impact of Knowledge Graphs. Size matters and quantity can generate new qualities even given the fact that nobody can define the precise number from where on it happens (Hegel 1812). One related question is the distinction of knowledge bases and Knowledge Graphs. According to Akerkar and Sajja (2010), a *knowledge-based system* consists of two parts: a *knowledge base* containing the *knowledge* and an *inference engine* that can be used to derive new facts or answering questions over the knowledge base.[17] A further important characteristic of a knowledge base is the distinction between ABox and TBox; see Brachman and Schmolze (1985). An assertion box (ABox) contains a set of assertions/factual statements. The strictly separated terminological box (TBox) defines the terminology used by ABox statements and adds more general logical formulas using this terminology. It provides an intensional definition of potential infinitely many additional facts (derived by the inference engine). Knowledge Graphs may have quite a different architecture and structure. Logical formulas are missing, and the terminological knowledge is hosted at the same layer as the assertions, i.e., it is just several additional assertions and some graphs may even be working without them at all. This has two consequences:

- First, there is little to reason with a Knowledge Graph. In the case of schema.org-based Knowledge Graphs, it is usually a simple tool like Google's test tool for structured data[18] that enforces certain constraints on valid graphs.
- Second, a rigidly defined schema can be used to define user interfaces, to ensure data quality (correctness and completeness), and to allow optimization of storage, querying, maintenance, and transactions. These are the key success factors of relational databases (Codd 1970). However, such a rigid schema definition also introduces a severe bottleneck when it is about the need to integrate data from various, semi-structured, heterogeneous, and dynamic sources. The assumption of a rigidly defined structured, homogeneous, and stable schema breaks and make such data integration ineffective and non-scalable. Therefore, it is not a bug but a feature of Knowledge Graphs to be less strict in this respect than traditional data or knowledge bases.

---

[16]https://en.wikipedia.org/wiki/Semantic_network

[17]These facts are not really "new" but rather derived from intensional definitions using logical formulas that implicitly already contained them.

[18]https://search.google.com/structured-data/testing-tool

Google coined the term *Knowledge Graph* in 2012 to build a model of the world. Meanwhile, it has become a hype term in the product and service industry. Already in tourism,[19] not necessarily the most innovative area in general, every major player has a Knowledge Graph and thousands of players (such as destination management organizations) need or want one. The drive for this stems from the fact how increasingly important successful e-marketing and e-commerce have become in terms of the value distribution in tourism and other areas. In general, the current dynamics around Knowledge Graphs comes from the economic sector and not from the scientific community. So, a simple definition could be that it is a trendy term to phrase and guide current data (and service) integration problems. It is not the first and most likely not the last approach tackling this very hard problem. However, it is also the first time that we approach this problem on a worldwide scale.

The *knowledge acquisition bottleneck* (cf. Feigenbaum 1984; Hoekstra 2010) caused the AI winter[20] around 40 years ago. Seeing it solved by millions of people that hack billions of statements in the Knowledge Graph (i.e., Semantic Web) is an interesting experience (Fensel and Musen 2001). If we would have proposed this as a solution around 1980, people would have kicked us out of universities immediately. Even Douglas Lenat's vision (Lenat and Guha 1989) to generate the solution with 50 employees looks rather small compared to this solution. Meanwhile we have a Semantic Web based on schema.org that is used by more than 1.2 billion web pages hosting more than 38 billion semantic statements.[21]

What is especially amazing is that it is done at a *factual* level instead of using some logical expressions as shortcuts for potential billions of statements. A knowledge base is built by writing down billions of facts. Facts are enumerated like describing a set extensionally instead of intensionally. Like one would replace the proof by induction by proofs for 1, then for 2, then for 3, and so on. Maybe this is just due to the early stage of the development of the Knowledge Graph? Maybe it will be the machines that take over this task. Unfortunately, they may not use logic and may produce shortcuts we are no longer able to understand. Similarly, machine and deep learning methods will increasingly be used for the construction, refinement, and enrichment of a Knowledge Graph (Paulheim 2018a). Various ways to combine inductive and deductive techniques have already been deeply investigated in the LarKC project which has been aiming to apply reasoning on the Semantic Web given its size, heterogeneity, semi-structured character, and velocity; see Fensel and van Harmelen (2007), Fensel et al. (2008). The underlying assumptions of traditional

---

[19]Note that tourism is one of the most important economical verticals on a worldwide scale, accounting for around 10% of the global GDP and total employment in 2017 (WTTC 2018).

[20]https://en.wikipedia.org/wiki/AI_winter

[21]Web Data Commons—RDFa, Microdata, Embedded JSON-LD, and Microformats Data Sets, November 2017. http://webdatacommons.org/structureddata/2017-12/stats/stats.html. Guha et al. (2016) reports that 31% of all pages from a sample of 10 billion web pages are using schema.org. The most recent crawl reports more than 30 billion quads finding more than 37% semantically annotated web sites of around 32 pay-level domains. http://webdatacommons.org/structureddata/2018-12/stats/stats.html

logic with small axiom sets, 100% correctness and completeness, and static character of the knowledge break at the scale of the web or large Knowledge Graphs. In fact, Wahlster pointed out in one of his recent talks the proper combination of inductive and deductive, knowledge-based approaches as a key challenge for future research on Artificial Intelligence.[22] This holds especially for work on the Internet of Things which is a network of physical devices, vehicles, home appliances, and other items embedded with electronics, software, sensors, actuators, and connectivity which enables these things to connect, collect, and exchange data and start to act beyond the virtual world.[23]

Summing up the discussion we could state that Knowledge Graphs are *very* large semantic nets that integrate various and heterogeneous information sources to represent knowledge about certain domains of discourse. How they can be built and used will be discussed in the following sections.[24]

1.3   An Empirical Definition of Knowledge Graphs

Below we give a survey on open and proprietary Knowledge Graphs with their definitions and important characteristics graphs (cf. Paulheim 2017 and furthers).[25] We order these approaches by the years they were first released.

1.3.1   Open Knowledge Graphs

The research on Semantic Web and linked data led to many open datasets eventually to comprise the Linked Open Data cloud (see Sect. 2.5). These datasets are now mostly rebranded as Knowledge Graphs. These Knowledge Graphs are typically cross-domain. Many open Knowledge Graphs are sourced from Wikipedia since it contains a very large factual knowledge spread over multiple domains. Some Knowledge Graphs also benefited from unstructured corpus, lexicon, Ontologies, and crowdsourcing for their building process. In this section, we introduce some of the prominent open Knowledge Graphs.

DBpedia[26] (Auer et al. 2007; Lehmann et al. 2015) is a Knowledge Graph first published in 2007. It is the de facto central dataset on the Semantic Web (also

---

[22]Professor Wahlster's Keynote: 30 Jahre DFKI—Von der Idee zum Markterfolg, at the event "30 Jahre DFKI—KI für den Menschen", Berlin, Oktober 17, 2018.

[23]https://en.wikipedia.org/wiki/Internet_of_things

[24]One could also call it *Knowledge Web* as proposed in Fensel et al. (1997).

[25]See Noy et al. (2019) for more details on the Knowledge Graphs of Bing (Microsoft), eBay, Facebook, Google, and IBM Watson.

[26]http://dbpedia.org/

referred to as "nucleus") since it is linked to many other datasets. The Knowledge Graph is predominantly extracted from the structured data on Wikipedia pages (mostly infoboxes), via extractors that can be tuned for extracting different kinds of data. The DBpedia Knowledge Graph is built on top of the crowd-maintained DBpedia Ontology (specified in OWL) that is mapped from the infobox metadata of Wikipedia. The Knowledge Graph is published following the Semantic Web standards as RDF dumps and SPARQL endpoints. DBpedia is released periodically but also offers a live endpoint synchronized with Wikipedia.[27] The October 2016 release contains 13B RDF triples. The DBpedia Ontology contains 760 classes and about 3000 properties.[28] DBpedia has many application areas such as Natural Language Processing and knowledge exploration and enrichment.

Freebase[29] (Bollacker et al. 2008) was a collaborative knowledge base launched in 2007. The company that run Freebase was bought by Google in 2010, and since then, the knowledge base has improved Google's Knowledge Graph. Freebase was shut down by Google in 2016 and its knowledge has been incrementally included in Wikidata. The latest dump contained 1.9B facts.[30] Freebase had its own custom data model that supported local properties.

YAGO[31] (Suchanek et al. 2007; Hoffart et al. 2013; Mahdisoltani et al. 2015) is another Knowledge Graph built based on Wikipedia content, first released in 2008. YAGO fuses entities extracted from Wikipedia articles with WordNet synsets to enrich the type hierarchy. The main difference between YAGO and DBpedia is that YAGO Ontology only extracts a handful number of relations and focuses on keeping the Knowledge Graph compact but highly accurate and consistent. YAGO uses an extended version of RDFS as formalism. YAGO2 improves the initial knowledge base with geospatial and temporal information and YAGO3 focuses on multilingualism and integrates data from Wikidata. YAGO currently contains 120M facts and 350K classes.[32]

NELL[33] (Carlson et al. 2010; Mitchell et al. 2018) builds a cross-domain knowledge base with machine learning methods based on 500 million web pages. It uses a predefined initial Ontology to determine the types of relations that need to be extracted from the web. NELL agents run continuously and keep improving the knowledge base by creating new facts and delete obsolete and wrong ones. NELL

---

[27]https://wiki.dbpedia.org/online-access/DBpediaLive

[28]https://wiki.dbpedia.org/develop/datasets/dbpedia-version-2016-10

[29]http://www.freebase.com/

[30]https://developers.google.com/freebase/

[31]https://www.mpi-inf.mpg.de/departments/databases-and-information-systems/research/yago-naga/yago/downloads/

[32]https://www.mpi-inf.mpg.de/departments/databases-and-information-systems/research/yago-naga/yago/

[33]See http://rtw.ml.cmu.edu/rtw/resources and http://rtw.ml.cmu.edu/rtw/kbbrowser/

agents run since 2010 and the knowledge base currently contains over 2.7M facts.[34] The NELL knowledge base uses a simple frame-based formalism, and the knowledge base is provided as a big tab-separated value file. Some researchers mapped NELL data model to RDF and OWL (Giménez-García et al. 2018).

Wikidata[35] (Vrandečić and Krötzsch 2014) is a community curated Knowledge Graph and a sister project of Wikipedia, launched in 2012. Like DBpedia, it is based on the knowledge of Wikipedia but can be also edited by community members. In fact, Wikidata and Wikipedia may have a two-way relationship, meaning the facts from Wikidata can be used to enrich Wikipedia articles. The main characteristics of Wikidata is that it focuses on provenance and context of the data. For instance, population of a city is not given as a binary relation only, but also with context information such as "according to the measurement done by a certain statistics organization." Wikidata has a customized data model that supports qualifiers and context information, but they also provide mappings to RDF and OWL (Erxleben et al. 2014). For accessing the Knowledge Graph, Wikidata provides RDF dumps and SPARQL endpoints; however, querying is more complicated due to the data model that supports n-ary relationships.[36] The Knowledge Graph contains more than 65M entities.[37] The RDF representation contains more than 7B triples in August 2019.[38]

KBpedia[39] (Bergman 2018) is a knowledge base that contains mappings to Wikipedia, Wikidata, schema.org, DBpedia, GeoNames, OpenCyc, and UMBEL. Its main purpose is to support AI applications, for instance, through enabling training set generation[40] for machine learning. The knowledge base was launched in 2016 and made open source in 2018. KBpedia is published using OWL 2 formalism and contains 55,000 concepts, 5000 properties, and 70 mostly disjoint typologies in its base model to ease the modularization of the knowledge base. The knowledge base claims to have 98% coverage of Wikidata and consequently to contain 45M instances.[41]

Datacommons.org[42] is an open Knowledge Graph launched by Google in 2018 that integrates several public sources and contains mainly knowledge about

---

[34]Last access: August 2019. NELL extracts millions of beliefs, but "facts" are only the beliefs with a confidence value higher than 0.9.

[35]https://www.wikidata.org/wiki/Wikidata:Main_Page

[36]The complexity can be overcome by writing queries over the "truthy graph"; see the examples in https://www.wikidata.org/wiki/Wikidata:SPARQL_query_service/queries

[37]https://www.wikidata.org/wiki/Wikidata:News

[38]As the result of COUNT SPARQL query showed on https://query.wikidata.org. The statistics regarding the number of statements shows that in April 2018, Wikidata contained more than 400M statements (Malyshev et al. 2018). This big difference is because of the fact that a statement in Wikidata can be represented with multiple RDF triples due to the need for reification.

[39]http://www.kbpedia.org/

[40]http://kbpedia.org/use-cases

[41]2.10 release.

[42]http://datacommons.org/

geographic and administrative areas, demographics, and other publicly available data such as weather and real estate. There is no public information regarding the formalism and size of the Knowledge Graph; however, the facts are represented in forms of triples with a provenance value attached to each fact. Another indication regarding the formalism is that it uses the schema.org vocabulary for describing things and extends the vocabulary slightly. The Knowledge Graph does not provide dumps, but it is accessible via a browser interface and a Python API.

1.3.2   Proprietary Knowledge Graphs

Various Knowledge Graphs have been developed by companies to enable their customers' applications. In this section, we will briefly introduce some of those Knowledge Graphs and their purposes.

Cyc[43] (Lenat and Guha 1989; Lenat 1995) is one of the longest-living AI projects and a common-sense knowledge base. Its initial release dates to 1984. Cyc knowledge base contains 1.5M concepts, 20M general axioms, and domain-specific extensions for various areas such as healthcare, transportation, and financial services. Cyc's content is curated by Cyccorp, but it adopts tools and methods to retrieve knowledge from external sources when necessary. The knowledge base is represented with the CycL language, a frame-based language that is expressive beyond first-order logic.[44] Cyc benefits from microtheories (Guha 1991) for efficient reasoning and avoiding inconsistencies that may otherwise occur in a large knowledge base. The knowledge base contains a variety of knowledge from general knowledge such as "Causes start at or before the time that their effects start" to highly domain-specific knowledge such as stock prices. Cyc knowledge base and supporting applications are proprietary; however, a research license for noncommercial use can be obtained. A fragment of Cyc was published in RDF format for public use as OpenCyc until 2017, but it is no longer released.

Facebook's Entities Graph[45] is maintained by Facebook and used internally to support the graph search functionality. It was initially launched in 2010 and contains knowledge about the Facebook users, namely, their profile information, interests, and connections. The Knowledge Graph is accessible via the Facebook Graph API. The Knowledge Graph contains 500M facts (Noy et al. 2019).

Google's Knowledge Graph[46] was launched in 2012 initially to improve Google's search engine results, effectively converting Google to a question-answering engine. In October 2016, Google announced that the Knowledge Graph

---

[43]http://www.cyc.com/

[44]Technical report from February 2019: https://cyc.com/cyc-technology-overview

[45]http://www.facebook.com/notes/facebook-engineering/under-the-hood-the-entities-graph/10151490531588920

[46]https://developers.google.com/knowledge-graph/

holds over 70B facts (Noy et al. 2019).[47] There is no public documentation regarding the underlying technology and formalism of the Knowledge Graph, but it is known that the standard schema.org types are used to describe the things in the graph. Google integrates data from several sources in their Knowledge Graph, such as Wikipedia, World Bank, Eurostat, etc. Additionally, they utilize schema.org annotations and data from the web. The Google Knowledge Graph currently also powers the Google Assistant (see Footnote 47). The Knowledge Graph is accessible via the Google Knowledge Graph API.

Yahoo!'s Knowledge Graph[48] (Blanco et al. 2013) was launched in 2013. The Knowledge Graph acquires data from heterogenous sources and fuses them under a common OWL Ontology. The fusing process includes reconciliation and cleaning of knowledge. The core of the Knowledge Graph is the data from Wikipedia. It is then enriched with sources like MusicBrainz and some commercial data providers. During the Knowledge Graph building process, machine learning methods and template-based methods are utilized. The common Ontology contains 300 classes and 1300 properties (see Footnote 48). Yahoo! utilizes the Knowledge Graph to solve tasks like search, relationship discovery, and natural language processing tasks.

Knowledge Vault[49] (Dong et al. 2014a) is a research project acquired by Google that aims to create a large probabilistic knowledge base extracted from different kinds of web content and data. They fuse knowledge from four different sources, such as unstructured text, HTML DOM trees, HTML tables, and schema.org annotations. The extracted triples are validated against existing Knowledge Graphs (e.g., Freebase) in order to increase the reliability of the facts. At the time the work (Dong et al. 2014a) was published (2014), the Knowledge Vault contained over 270M facts.

---

[47]https://www.businessinsider.de/why-google-assistant-will-win-the-ai-race-2016-10?r=US&IR=T

[48]https://www.slideshare.net/NicolasTorzec/the-yahoo-knowledge-graph

[49]https://ai.google/research/pubs/pub45634

Chapter 2
How to Build a Knowledge Graph

Abstract This chapter outlines the state of the art of Knowledge Graph technologies by introducing the process of building a Knowledge Graph. We define the following major steps of an overall process model: (1) knowledge creation, (2) knowledge hosting, (3) knowledge curation, and (4) knowledge deployment. We demonstrate the methodology for the knowledge creation process that creates, extracts, and structures the fact base for a Knowledge Graph. We describe the process of knowledge collection, storage, and retrieval that implements established knowledge in a graph-based storage system. We analyze existing methods and tools to improve the quality of a large Knowledge Graph. For the Knowledge Curation process, we establish sub-steps, such as knowledge assessment, cleaning, and enrichment. For each of them, we determine various categories and dimensions that have been developed and described in the literature and identify tasks which can be applied (e.g., Knowledge Graph completion and correctness, error detection and correction, identifying and resolving duplicates). Finally, we describe the deployment process of a Knowledge Graph based on the following principles: findability, accessibility, interoperability, and reusability.

2.1 Introduction

According to Gómez-Pérez et al. (2017), Knowledge Graph technologies consist of:

- Knowledge representation and reasoning (languages, schema, and standard vocabularies)
- Knowledge storage (graph databases and repositories)
- Knowledge engineering (methodologies, editors and design patterns)
- Knowledge learning, including schema learning and population

This is true for knowledge-based systems. Knowledge Graph methods and techniques must additionally reflect the specific focus on vast amounts of instance data beyond any traditional knowledge base; see Schultz et al. (2012). We identify the following major steps (see Fig. 2.1) in an overall process model. A more detailed task model is provided in Fig. 2.2.

© Springer Nature Switzerland AG 2020

D. Fensel et al., *Knowledge Graphs*, https://doi.org/10.1007/978-3-030-37439-6_2

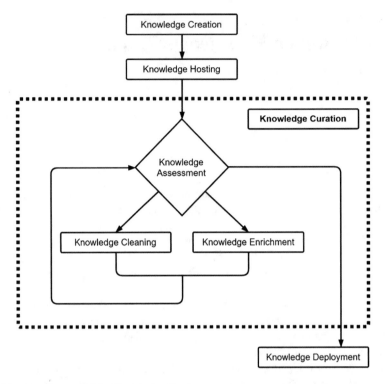

Fig. 2.1 A process model for Knowledge Graph generation

- A traditional knowledge acquisition (or maybe better-called knowledge engineer-ing)[1] phase that establishes the core data for a Knowledge Graph (see Sect. 2.2).
- The process to implement this knowledge in a proper storage system such as a document or graph-based repository (see Sect. 2.3).
- The knowledge curation process (cf. Paulheim 2017) establishes large Knowl-edge Graphs of significant coverage and quality. As sub-steps of this curation process, we identify the following activities: knowledge assessment, cleaning, and enrichment (see Sect. 2.4).
- Finally, we need to deploy and apply such a Knowledge Graph (see Sect. 2.5).

Each of the mentioned steps is discussed in detail during the following sub-sections. Similar models can be found, for example, in Gawriljuk et al. (2016), Kejriwal et al. (2017), and Villazón-Terrazas et al. (2017).[2]

---

[1]A forgotten debate on whether knowledge is elicited or constructed.

[2]A framework for the large-scale integration of publicly available information on points of interest (POI)—that is highly relevant for the touristic area—is described in Athanasiou et al. (2019a, b). See more details on the data integration work bench at the SLIPO website http://slipo.eu/

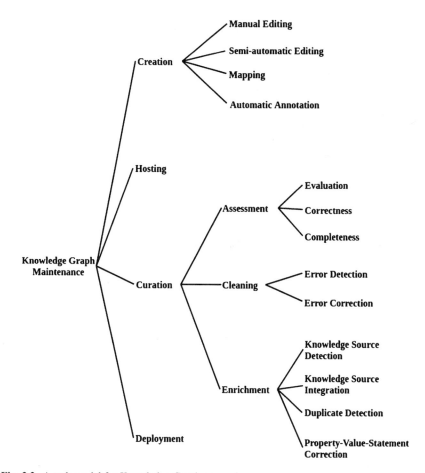

Fig. 2.2 A task model for Knowledge Graph generation

2.2   Knowledge Creation

Knowledge acquisition describes the process of extracting information from different sources, structuring it, and creating useful knowledge; see Schreiber et al. (2000). Knowledge could be represented differently among systems, such as text documents, web pages, relation databases, and databases. A way to overcome this data representation discrepancy and provide the data in a structured way is provided by semantic data. In this section, we introduce our methodology, our modeling language, and an extensive collection of tools that support the generation of formalized knowledge.

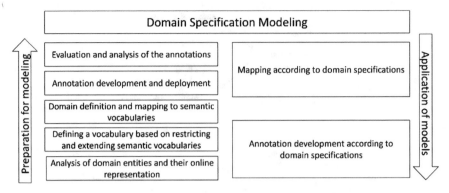

Fig. 2.3 Methodology for semantic annotation (Panasiuk et al. 2018a)

2.2.1   Knowledge Creation Methodology

In Fig. 2.3 our methodology for semantic annotation is shown. The methodology consists of three main parts:

1. The bottom-up part, which describes the steps of a first annotation process
2. The domain specification modeling that reflects these results
3. The top-down part, which applies the constructed models to further knowledge acquisition

The *bottom-up* part of the methodology describes the annotation process in a new domain and includes the following steps:

1. *Analysis of domain entities and their online representation:* First, to start the process of knowledge acquisition, we define a domain area (e.g., tourism) that needs to be covered. The study of the domain includes the analysis of the touristic real-world entities and extraction of the existing relevant service types. Second, we identify the types of web pages, databases, or APIs and detect the format and type of data they provide. With domain analysis, we find out what data are suitable and essential for the annotation process.
2. *Definition of a vocabulary based on restricting and extending semantic vocabularies:* A vital element of a Knowledge Graph is the Ontology (see Studer et al. 1998; Staab and Studer 2010) it uses. It allows us to describe and represent all the information in semantic annotations. For our purpose, we use schema.org as a de facto standard for semantic annotations, launched in 2011 by Google, Yahoo!, Bing, and Yandex (Guha 2011).
3. *Domain specifications and mapping to the semantic vocabularies*: For selected service types, we determine the best way to map them to schema.org vocabulary correctly, i.e., to choose the right type with properties and ranges. If there are no suitable types or properties, then we define a list of extensions (Guha et al. 2016).
4. *Annotation development and deployment:* To annotate content from a source, we use the content data structure. If the content is arranged with a structured data

format, then the annotation can be performed automatically (given that the mappings are defined). If not, then a manual or semi-automatic annotation needs to be done. This step must be supported by tools, such as annotation editors, wrappers, mapping tools, and an evaluator.

5. *Evaluation and analysis of the annotations:* After the annotations are deployed, we regularly monitor their impact on search engine results, especially rich results[3] on Google Search. For quantitative evaluations, it is good to use Google's Search Console, with which it is possible to measure how much time was required to detect the annotated pages, how often the annotated pages were crawled, and how many errors were detected. For qualitative evaluations, the monitoring of Google's search engine results is suitable, especially the appearances of rich results.

The *domain specifications modeling* focuses on developing domain-specific patterns which we call domain specifications (DS) (Şimşek et al. 2018a). We will elaborate on them in the following subsection.

The *top-down* part of the methodology describes the annotation process in case the modeling effort for a specific domain has already been done and includes the following steps:

1. *Mapping according to domain specifications:* In this step, we can map incoming data to developed domain specifications using predefined mapping rules.
2. *Annotation development according to domain specifications:* This step is based on these predefined domain specifications that are translated into a form interface fostering manual and semi-automatic knowledge acquisition process.

2.2.2 Our Modelling Language

The use of semantic annotations has experienced a tremendous surge since the introduction of schema.org (Guha 2011). Schema.org was launched by major search engines Bing, Google, Yahoo!, and Yandex in 2011 as an Ontology (Studer et al. 1998; Staab and Studer 2010) to empower web search on a global scale. The schema. org vocabulary, along with the Microdata, RDFa, or JSON-LD formats, is used to mark up website content. Schema.org relies on a flexible and cross-domain data model and is organized hierarchically. Schema.org initially contained 297 classes and 187 relations, which over the time have grown to 598 types, 862 properties, and 114 enumeration values (Guha et al. 2016). The provided corpus of types (e.g., LocalBusiness, SkiResort, Restaurant), properties (e.g., name, description, address), range definitions (e.g., Text, URL, PostalAddress), and enumeration values (e.g., DayOfWeek, EventStatusType, ItemAvailability) cover a large number of different domains, including the tourism area. The data model of schema.org defines a

---

[3]For example, rich snippets, https://en.wikipedia.org/wiki/Google_Searchology. See also Sect. 3.2.

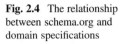

Fig. 2.4 The relationship between schema.org and domain specifications

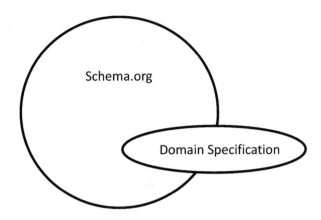

multiple inheritance hierarchy for properties and types. Also, instances can be elements of several types. The domain and range of properties are not formally defined. There is no type definition based on axioms but only some subclass hierarchy.

Schema.org has become a de facto standard for annotating data (Mika 2015). Such markup can be recognized by search engines and different automated agents (e.g., chatbots or personal assistant systems) and improve information access. Schema.org is the broadest vocabulary, which is used by more than a quarter of the web pages (Guha et al. 2016). Schema.org annotations are an apparent basis for building a Knowledge Graph.

A domain specification, i.e., our design patterns for semantic annotations, is an *extended subset* of types, properties, and ranges from schema.org (Şimşek et al. 2018a); see Fig. 2.4. We restrict schema.org to proper subsets as it is an approach for covering any type of resource, and we need a specific focus. We may need to extend schema.org as it mostly aims at web search and covers many domains in a shallow way, whereas we may need more details for specific tasks and domains. Through the restricted focus, we can make stronger conceptual commitments. This is also in sync with schema.org that "can at best hope to provide the core for the most common topics" (Guha et al. 2016). Also, it provides the notion of external extensions to add more domain and task-specific details.[4]

The goal of a domain specification is to give a model of how a domain should be represented in a semantically structured way. It will help to improve the completeness and correctness of the annotation process for a given domain. In the end, domain specifications are design patterns (Gamma et al. 1995) for developing proper semantic annotations, either with pure schema.org or together with its extensions. A formal definition of domain specification (abstract syntax and formal semantics) are provided in Appendix.

---

[4]https://schema.org/docs/extension.html

To annotate, for example, a hotel, we need to select a collection of properties and ranges to cover the content of a hotel web page. Schema.org (see Fig. 2.5) gives a list of possible properties and ranges for hotel annotation. We need to analyze hotel content, locate all relevant information presented on a page, and then according to this, define types, properties, and ranges from schema.org to represent available information. The following list describes properties and ranges for annotating a hotel with the type *Hotel* from schema.org:

1. *aggregateRating* describes the overall rating of a hotel and is essential for rich snippet representation. It is based on a collection of reviews or ratings of the hotel. The property has *AggregateRating* type in its range.
2. *availableLanguage* shows the information about which languages are spoken by hotel service staff. The range of the property is *Text*, but the text information should be presented in the form of language codes from the IETF BCP 47 standard.[5]
3. *checkinTime* shows the earliest time when someone may check into a hotel.
4. *checkoutTime* shows the latest time when someone may check out of a hotel.
5. *contactPoint* describes the contact information of a hotel, based on specific contact types. The range of this property is the type *ContactPoint*.
6. *containsPlace* shows what other places are included in the hotel, e.g., bar, restaurant, or spa. The range of this property is the types *Place* and *Accommodation* as well as their subtypes.
7. *currenciesAccepted* shows what currencies are accepted by the hotel. The range of the property is Text, but the text information should be presented in ISO 4217 currency format.[6]
8. *description* contains information that describes the hotel and its facilities. The range of the property is *Text*.
9. *email* shows the email of the hotel. The range of the property is *Text*.
10. *faxNumber* gives the fax number of the hotel. The range of the property is *Text*.
11. *founder* gives the name of the person who founded the hotel. The range of the property is *Person*.
12. *name* presents the name of the hotel. The range of the property is *Text*.
13. *foundingDate* shows the information as to when the hotel was founded. The range of the property is *Date*.
14. *geo* gives the geo-coordinates of the hotel. The range *GeoCoordinates* specifies the latitude and longitude of the location.
15. *hasMap* gives a *URL* to a map of the place.
16. *image* describes the available images on the web page. This can be a URL or a fully described ImageObject with information about the size and caption of the image.

---

[5] https://tools.ietf.org/html/bcp47

[6] https://en.wikipedia.org/wiki/ISO_4217

Hotel

Thing > Organization > LocalBusiness > LodgingBusiness > Hotel
Thing > Place > LocalBusiness > LodgingBusiness > Hotel

A hotel is an establishment that provides lodging paid on a short-term basis
(Source: Wikipedia, the free encyclopedia, see http://en.wikipedia.org
/wiki/Hotel).
See also the dedicated document on the use of schema.org for marking up
hotels and other forms of accommodations.

Property	Expected Type	Description
Properties from LodgingBusiness		
amenityFeature	LocationFeature Specification	An amenity feature (e.g. a characteristic or service) of the Accommodation. This generic property does not make a statement about whether the feature is included in an offer for the main accommodation or available at extra costs.
audience	Audience	An intended audience, i.e. a group for whom something was created. Supersedes serviceAudience.
availableLanguage	Language or Text	A language someone may use with or at the item, service or place. Please use one of the language codes from the IETF BCP 47 standard. See also inLanguage
checkinTime	DateTime or Time	The earliest someone may check into a lodging establishment.
checkoutTime	DateTime or Time	The latest someone may check out of a lodging establishment.
numberOfRooms	Number or QuantitativeValue	The number of rooms (excluding bathrooms and closets) of the

Fig. 2.5 Properties and ranges for the schema.org type *Hotel*

17. *makesOffer* describes the items, such as *HotelRoom*, *Suite*, and *Accommodation*, offered by a hotel. The type range *Offer* shows information about the availability of itemOffered and its name, price, and so forth.
18. *openingHoursSpecification* shows the opening hours of the hotel. The property has type range *OpeningHoursSpecification* with its properties, e.g., *closes, dayOfWeek,* and *opens.*
19. *paymentAccepted* shows what kind of payment is accepted by the hotel, e.g., cash, credit card, etc.
20. *petsAllowed* indicates whether pets are allowed to enter the hotel. The property has the ranges *Text* or *Boolean.*
21. *photo* represents some photos of the hotel. The property has type *ImageObject* as range.
22. *priceRange* specifies the price range of the hotel, for example, "$$$". The property has the type *Text* as its range.
23. *review* describes the reviews of the selected hotel. The property has the type *Review* as range.
24. *sameAs* shows the URL of external reference web pages. For example, the URL of the hotels' Wikipedia page, social media page, or official website.
25. *starRating* presents an official rating for a hotel, e.g., from national associations or standards bodies. The property has the type range *Rating.*
26. *telephone* is the telephone number of a hotel. The property has range *Text,* but the text should be in the appropriate format.
27. *url* shows the URL of the hotel.

Throughout this section, we pointed out that schema.org covers many domains in a generic manner and we create extended subsets (i.e., domain-specific patterns) to make it more suitable for specific domains and tasks. The community has already been acting toward providing external extensions for schema.org, and these extensions can be adopted alongside core schema.org to create domain-specific patterns. Two prominent examples come from the retail domain. Schema.org contains types and properties for product descriptions and offers, however, only very generically. In fact, there are only two types, namely, product and service, that do not have any subtypes for more specific products and services and their properties. There are however product classification standards already established that provide a relatively deep taxonomy and a rich set of properties. Stolz and Hepp propose a generic and elegant way to incorporate such taxonomies with schema.org in order to make it more suitable for describing product and services (Stolz and Hepp 2018). They provide a deterministic way to create URNs based on the internal type and property identifiers of widely adopted product classification standards such as eCl@ss[7] and UNSPC.[8] They provide additionalType and additionalProperty properties to attach external type and property identifiers to entities annotated with schema.org. This

---

[7]https://eclass.eu

[8]United Nations Standard Products and Services Code—https://unspc.org

way, for instance, in the case of retail, product, and service descriptions can be enriched with types and properties from eCl@ss which contains over 45K product classes and 19K properties,[9] as well as from UNSPC which contains over 150K classes in its taxonomy. An example of using PCS classes and properties with schema.org is the annotation of a notebook computer. Schema.org does neither have a specific notebook type nor a property for, let us say, battery capacity. A URN (urn:pcs:eclass:11.0.0:c:AEI956008) based on the internal identifier of note-book class in eCl@ss standard (AEI956008) is generated and attached to the Product annotation with additionalType property. In the same fashion, a URN (urn:pcs: eclass:11.0.0:c:02-AAR570) for "battery capacity" property is generated and attached to the same annotation via additionalProperty property.[10]

Similarly, GS1, a nonprofit organization that maintains many business standards including the widely adopted barcode standard, provides a rich vocabulary[11] to improve product search on the web. Unlike the aforementioned extension method, they provide a complete external vocabulary integrated with the schema.org hierar-chy.[12] They extend schema.org with 43 types and 358 properties. For example, they extend the Product type with a subtype WearableProduct which itself has Footwear as subtype. A footwear retailer can use these new types to describe its products in a more domain-specific way than by the core schema.org.

2.2.3   Knowledge Generation Tools

The properties and ranges described in Sect. 2.2.2 give an overview of what properties and ranges users need to annotate a hotel. Figure 2.6 demonstrates the output file of the hotel annotation process. In order to support the semantic annota-tion process, tools are required for manual and semi-automatic editing, mappings of external schemas, automatic annotation, and finally, evaluation (validation and verification).[13]

2.2.3.1   Manual Editing

The annotation process of web content can be done manually via the semantify.it[14] Annotation Editor (Kärle et al. 2017). The interface will be generated automatically based on the domain specifications; see Fig. 2.7. In order to start a new manual

---

[9]Release v11.0—https://wiki.eclass.eu/wiki/Category:Products

[10]See Stolz and Hepp (2018) for a full JSON-LD example based on a previous version of eCl@ss.

[11]https://gs1.org/standards/gs1-smartsearch

[12]The integration is realized through the mechanisms provided by SKOS and RDFS.

[13]See also Uren et al. (2006) and Gómez-Pérez et al. (2010).

[14]https://semantify.it/

Ferienhof Hotel Garni Oblasser ✕

```json
{
  "@context": "http://schema.org",
  "@type": [
    "Hotel"
  ],
  "url": [
    "http://www.ferienhof-oblasser.at",
    "http://maps.mayrhofen.at/?foreignResource=C5EC2DF7-5E30-42AB-9D58-
5607FB343ECA"
  ],
  "address": {
    "@type": "PostalAddress",
    "name": "Oblasser, Ferienhof",
    "streetAddress": "Hochstegen 835",
    "addressLocality": "Mayrhofen",
    "postalCode": "6290",
    "addressCountry": "AT",
    "telephone": "0043 5285 64666",
    "faxNumber": "0043 5285 64559",
    "email": "info@ferienhof-oblasser.at",
    "url": "http://www.ferienhof-oblasser.at"
  },
  "name": "Ferienhof Hotel Garni Oblasser",
  "description": [

"Children up to the age of 6 go free, up to the age of 12 a 50%
price reduction.\nIncludes: Heating, garage, water, electricity,
local taxes and bed linen.\nExcludes: final cleaning charge",
```

Fig. 2.6 Example of hotel annotation in JSON-LD format

annotation, the user selects a domain specification, on which the annotation will be based, and gets the corresponding editing interface. If all required fields are filled in, the user gets presented with the annotation source code in JSON-LD format. This source code can then either be copy-pasted or stored on the semantify.it platform for further usage. The Annotation Editor can be used by users to annotate their web content and make the semantic annotation process easier, complete, and consistent.

Annotate Restaurant

ⓘ **name**   AKROPOLIS

ⓘ **description**   Wir heißen Sie herzlich im Restaurant AKROPOLIS willkommen!

ⓘ **url**   https://akropolis-innsbruck.com/

ⓘ **telephone**   +43 512 57 57 61

ⓘ **email**   contact@akropolis-innsbruck.com

ⓘ **address**
    ⓘ **addressCountry**
        ⓘ **name**   Österreich

    ⓘ **addressLocality**   Innsbruck

    ⓘ **addressRegion**   Tirol

    ⓘ **postalCode**   6020

    ⓘ **streetAddress**   Inrain 13

ⓘ 🚫 **aggregateRating**
    ⓘ **bestRating**   5

    ⓘ **ratingCount**   1

    ⓘ **ratingValue**   5

ⓘ 🚫 **acceptsReservations**   URL ∨   https://bda.bookatable.com/

Fig. 2.7 semantify.it Annotation Editor

2.2.3.2   Semi-automatic Editing

Semi-automatic support helps users to fill in the fields in the editor by extracting information from the given URI or source file. The user will need to select a domain specification and enter the URL of a web page or attach the source file, which he wants to annotate. If a source file is semi-structured, then the editor will suggest the mapping to JSON-LD by using the mappings as an approximation based on the training data. If the content is unstructured, some approaches to extract information from a web page can be applied. The information can be extracted from the source web page by tracking the appropriate HTML tags, such as title, sub-title, bold, italic, underlined, big character, keywords, lists, images, URLs, paragraph tags, and the associated full text. Some Ontology discovery techniques for the tourism domain are discussed in Karoui et al. (2004). The tree-based technique using the document object model (DOM)[15] of a web page is described in Gupta et al. (2003). Also, semantic types and properties can be automatically inferred through trained machine learning models (Gupta et al. 2012).

2.2.3.3   Mapping

Manual and semi-automatic editing only scales for small sets of static data. Large and fast-changing datasets require other methods to generate annotations effectively and continuously. The data are often provided by different institutions and might be in different formats and using different conceptual structures. To make this data accessible in a Knowledge Graph, we need to transfer it into the format and schema of our knowledge representation formalism. The conversation process is called data lifting (Villazón-Terrazas et al. 2017). There are many approaches and tools which cover data lifting from structured or semi-structured formats. The XLWrap approach generates graphs triples from specific cells of a spreadsheet (Langegger and Wöß 2009). The SLIPO toolkit supports lifting, interlinking, crawling, and fusing of geospatial datasets and will make their workbench open source available in the future (Athanasiou et al. 2019b). Mapping Master (M2) is a mapping language for converting spreadsheets to OWL (O'Connor et al. 2010). The XMLtoRDF tool provides a mapping document (XML document) that has a link between an XML Schema and an OWL Ontology (Van Deursen et al. 2008). Tripliser[16] is a Java library and command-line tool for creating triple graphs from XML. Also, GRDDL[17] translates the XML data into RDF. Virtuoso Sponger[18] generates Linked Data from a variety of data sources and supports a wide variety of data representation

---

[15]https://www.w3.org/DOM/

[16]http://daverog.github.io/tripliser/

[17]https://www.w3.org/TR/grddl/

[18]http://vos.openlinksw.com/owiki/wiki/VOS/VirtSponger

and serialization formats. R2RML[19] specifies how to translate relational data into the RDF format. RML (Dimou et al. 2014) extends R2RML's applicability to define mappings of data in other formats. With RML, rules can be expressed that map data with different structures and serializations (e.g., databases, XML or JSON data sources) to the domain-specific schema.org data model (cf. Şimşek et al. 2019a).

The semantify.it platform features a wrapper API where mappings can be stored and applied to corresponding data sources. The wrapper translates the data according to the mappings and stores it as JSON-LD in a MongoDB. From there, the data can be published on websites as annotations and optionally transferred to a Knowledge Graph. The platform offers an extension framework to store RML mappings. To store annotations for web services in the Knowledge Graph, the semantify.it platform provides a mapper/wrapper interface to translate the communication between an agent and an API (Şimşek et al. 2018b). This feature stores the respective information annotated with schema.org actions.[20] Semantify.it-actions takes into account the provenance of a data source and compares it with existing action mappings. If the data source already has an action mapping, the respective schema.org action description is attached to the instances mapped from the data source.

In Fig. 2.8 the Logical Source determines the input source that contains the data to be mapped. It consists of the reference to the input source, reference formulation, and iterator. The Subject Map describes how each triple's subject is generated and its type, in our case, schema.org types *Person* and *PostalAddress*. The Predicate-Object Map specifies how the triple's predicates and objects are generated. Figure 2.9 shows the input file in JSON format and Fig. 2.10 shows how the output will look after the mapping to schema.org by using RML mapping rules (Şimşek et al. 2019a).[21]

2.2.3.4   Automatic Annotation Tools

Automatic annotation tools extract data from the web using *natural language processing* (NLP) and *machine learning* (ML); see Cimiano et al. (2004). To extract knowledge from text and web pages, there exist various approaches, such as named entity recognition (Mohit 2014), information extraction (Chang et al. 2006), concept mining (Shehata et al. 2010), and text mining (Inzalkar and Sharma 2015). There are many tools or libraries available, such as GATE[22] for text analysis and language processing, OpenNLP[23] that supports the most common NLP tasks, and RapidMiner

---

[19]https://www.w3.org/TR/r2rml/

[20]Schema.org Actions provide means for describing web services.

[21]A special mapper implementation that can handle nested structures without joins. See Şimşek et al. (2019a) for details. See a new implementation that supports joins at https://github.com/semantifyit/RocketRML

[22]https://gate.ac.uk/

[23]https://opennlp.apache.org/

```
@prefix rr: <http://www.w3.org/ns/r2rml#> .
@prefix rml: <http://semweb.mmlab.be/ns/rml#> .
@prefix schema: <http://schema.org/> .
@prefix ql: <http://semweb.mmlab.be/ns/ql#> .
@base <http://sti2.at/> .

<#LOGICALSOURCE>
rml:source ".../exampleJSONtoSDO/input.json";
rml:referenceFormulation ql:JSONPath;
rml:baseSource <#Mapping>;
rml:iterator "$.*".
<#Mapping>
rml:logicalSource <#LOGICALSOURCE>;
 rr:subjectMap [
   rr:termType rr:BlankNode;
   rr:class schema:Person;
];
rr:predicateObjectMap [
   rr:predicate schema:name;
   rr:objectMap [ rml:reference "name" ];
];
rr:predicateObjectMap [
   rr:predicate schema:age;
   rr:objectMap [ rml:reference "age" ];
];
rr:predicateObjectMap [
   rr:predicate schema:address;
   rr:objectMap [
   rr:parentTriplesMap <#ADDRESSmapping>;
];
].
<#ADDRESSmapping>
rml:logicalSource <#LOGICALSOURCE>;
 rr:subjectMap [
   rr:termType rr:BlankNode;
   rr:class schema:PostalAddress;
 ];
rr:predicateObjectMap [
   rr:predicate schema:addressCountry;
   rr:objectMap [ rml:reference "livesIn.country" ];
];
rr:predicateObjectMap [
   rr:predicate schema:addressLocality;
   rr:objectMap [ rml:reference "livesIn.city" ];
].
```

Fig. 2.8 Example of RML mapping for type *Person* (with its properties *name, age*, and *address*) and type *PostalAddress* (with its properties *addressCountry* and *addressLocality*)

Fig. 2.9 Example of input (JSON)

```
[

{   "name":"Tom A.",
     "age":15,
     "livesIn":{
          "country":"Austria",
          "city":"Innsbruck"   }
  },
  {   "name":"Ralph S.",
      "age":25,
      "livesIn":{
          "country":"Austria",
          "city":"Vienna"    }
  },
  {   "name":"Anngelika B.",
      "age":77,
      "livesIn":{
          "country":"Germany",
          "city":"Munich"    }
  }

]
```

for data preparation, machine learning, deep learning, text mining, and predictive analytics; see Villazón-Terrazas et al. (2017). The typical tasks of NLP are Moschitti et al. (2017):

1. *Tokenization* is the process of transforming text into individual elements called tokens (e.g., words, keywords, phrases, or symbols).
2. *Stemming* is the process of reducing words into common to all its inflected variants called stems.
3. *Lemmatization* is the process of matching words with their canonical forms or dictionary forms called lemmas.
4. *Sentence boundary disambiguation* is the process of defining the beginning and end of a sentence in the text.
5. *Named entity recognition* (NER) or entity extraction is a subtask of information extraction that locates, classifies, and extracts named entities of a given type from an unstructured text. The NER task is domain dependent, and recognizers must be trained on the specific domains to recognize specific kinds of entities.
6. *Part-of-speech* (POS) *tagging* is the process of assigning parts of speech to words in a text, taking into account the characteristics and roles of the different parts of speech and the context around words.
7. *Chunking* is a process of attaching to POS tags additional information of the constituents of the sentence.

```
[
{ "@type": "http://schema.org/Person",
    "http://schema.org/name": "Tom A.",
    "http://schema.org/age": 15,
    "http://schema.org/address": {
            "@type": "http://schema.org/PostalAddress",
            "http://schema.org/addressCountry": "Austria",
            "http://schema.org/addressLocality": "Innsbruck"   }
},
{   "@type": "http://schema.org/Person",
    "http://schema.org/name": "Ralph S.",
    "http://schema.org/age": 25,
    "http://schema.org/address": {
            "@type": "http://schema.org/PostalAddress",
            "http://schema.org/addressCountry": "Austria",
            "http://schema.org/addressLocality": "Vienna"   }
},
{   "@type": "http://schema.org/Person",
    "http://schema.org/name": "Anngelika B.",
    "http://schema.org/age": 77,
    "http://schema.org/address": {
    "@type": "http://schema.org/PostalAddress",
    "http://schema.org/addressCountry": "Germany",
    "http://schema.org/addressLocality": "Munich"   }
}

]
```

Fig. 2.10 Example of output (JSON-LD)

8. *Syntactic parsing* is the process of detecting if the sentence is correct and provides the syntactic parse tree of the sentence, i.e., the syntactic structure of the sentence.
9. *Relation extraction* is a subtask of information extraction that discovers connections between entities in the text.
10. *Semantic role labeling* is the process of identifying the semantic roles in the sentence and assigning labels to words and phrases.
11. *Co-reference resolution* is the process of finding the expressions in a text referring to the same entities or things.

Automated annotation comes with a high training effort to adapt generic methods for specific domain and tasks. Only then a certain level of quality can be achieved. In general, if automated annotations would work, such annotations would no longer be needed as a machine could on the fly read and understand textual representations.

2.2.3.5 Evaluation

The work in Zaveri et al. (2016) introduces a quality assessment methodology to "evaluate the results of the knowledge engineering process." Criteria need to be introduced that define quality (e.g., accuracy, completeness, consistency, correctness, reliability, reusability) of these data. It helps to provide complete and correct knowledge representation of the entities to which it refers. More details are provided in Sect. 2.4, where we discuss this in the general context of knowledge cleaning.

Unlike most literature in the Knowledge Graph area, we have to define a severe distinction of the *validation* and the *verification* process (Panasiuk et al. 2019). The latter evaluates semantic annotations against a formal specification (e.g., schema definitions, integrity constraints). It is an internal check whether the semantic annotations conform with the formal requirements that define the golden standard for this evaluation. The former, i.e., validation, compares the semantic annotations with the web resource they annotate. Here the content, data, and services on the web provide the golden standard that is used to evaluate the quality of the semantic annotations. That is, we do not validate the correctness of the human-readable content of a web page but whether the found semantic annotations accurately describe them. For example, our evaluator does not make a robocall to find out whether the phone number of a hotel works and is the right one but only checks whether the semantic annotation and the content are consistent.[24]

The semantify.it evaluator is a web tool that offers the possibility to validate and verify schema.org annotations that are scraped from websites; see Fig. 2.11. The scraped annotations are verified against the schema.org vocabulary and domain specifications (Şimşek et al. 2018a) and for the compliance of annotations with integrity constraints. The domain specifications for the verification process can be selected by the user or semi-automatically provided by the tool based on the schema.org types of the evaluated annotation.

The verification process is executed in the backend, where irregularities are detected and presented through a formalized and structured report. It consists of:

1. The translation/normalization of the input annotation into a compacted JSON-LD document serialization, which is the format of choice for the verification process
2. The general verification of the annotation based on the Schema.org vocabulary
3. The domain-specific verification of the annotation based on the input domain specification
4. The creation of a verification report based on the detected errors

The first step ensures that the entities described by the schema.org annotation are represented as nested JSON objects in a syntactically correct way. By doing this, the following steps can rely on a recursive algorithm that checks every entity (nested JSON object) of the input annotations. During the general verification of the annotations, each entity is checked: the type(s), properties, and value types (ranges)

---

[24]https://techcrunch.com/2018/06/27/a-closer-look-at-google-duplex/?guccounter=1

2. Verification Report

⌄ Verification Result

Nr.	Type	Markup	View	Schema.org Verification	Domain-specific Verification
1	Event	jsonld	🔍	Conform with Warnings 🗎	Not Conform 🗎
2	BreadcrumbList	microdata	🔍	Conform ✓	No DS
3	PostalAddress	microdata	🔍	Conform with Warnings 🗎	No DS

⌄ Input

🌐   https://www.mayrhofen.at/events/detail/event/7-zillertaler-weisenblaesertreffen/

<>   <title>7. Zillertaler Weisenbläsertreffen : TVB Mayrhofen</title>
<meta name="description" content="<p class="MsoNormal"
style="margin: 0cm 0cm 12pt;">Teilnehmer: Ebbser Kaiserklang, Zillertaler
Weisenbläser, die Gfirmt'n, Klarinetten-Ensemble Zillertal">
<meta property="og:type" content="website">
<meta property="og:title" content="7. Zillertaler Weisenbläsertreffen : TVB

Fig. 2.11 semantify.it Verifier

of the nested JSON object must conform to the schema.org vocabulary. As for the domain-specific verification, the tree-like structures (data model of JSON) of the input domain specification and the input schema.org annotation make it easy to identify which nested JSON object of the domain specification belongs to which nested JSON object of the annotation. Each constraint defined by a domain specification node (represented by specific keywords and their values) is checked independently on its own. For this reason, the domain-specific verification algorithm is a recursive assertion of syntactic and semantic constraints for each entity (nested JSON object) of the input annotation. Any encountered irregularities are processed into a report.

The report contains detailed information about the detected errors; see Fig. 2.12 including error codes (ID of the error type), error titles, error severity, error paths (where within the annotation the error occurred), and textual descriptions of the errors. The validation of semantic annotations is the process of checking whether the semantic annotation corresponds to the content of the web page that it represents and if it is consistent with it. Semantic annotations should mark up the actual and visible information of a web page, correct links, images, and literal values without redundancy. The inaccurate representation of the resources can make semantic annotations useless for automated agents, cause an incorrect appearance in the search results, or make crawling and reasoning less useful for building applications on top of semantic annotations.

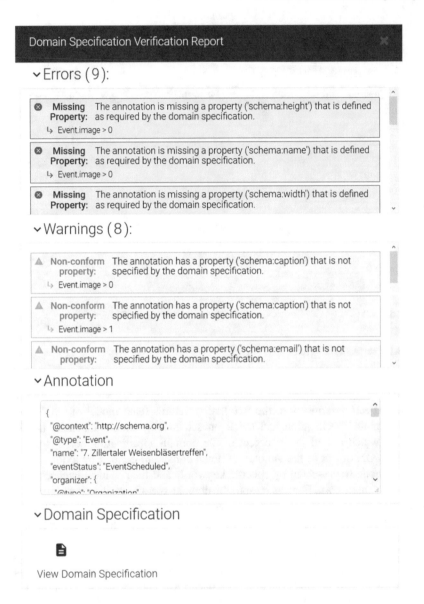

Fig. 2.12 semantify.it Verification Report

The errors during the annotation process may be caused by not following recommended guidelines,[25] e.g., structured data guidelines, insufficient expertise, technical or human errors (some of the issues can be detected by Google search

---

[25]https://developers.google.com/search/docs/guides/sd-policies

console[26]), or annotations not being in accordance with the content of web pages, so-called spammy structured markup.[27] The validation framework helps to detect inconsistencies between a web page and its annotations.

The validation of semantic annotations prevents the problem of penalizing the publisher of structured data by search engines for providing irrelevant information in the annotations and helps to get accurate information from automated agents and applications that use semantic annotations. The penalties may have undesired effects on a website (e.g., bad positioning of the website in search results) or even lead to a non-integration of the structured data (e.g., no generation of rich snippets).

Our framework ensures that all typical inconsistencies that can appear between schema.org annotations and content of a web page are discovered (e.g., a mismatch between URLs, text description in the annotation, and description on the web page). We provide a checking algorithm that compares extracted values from the annotations of a given web page to the content of this web page, taken from HTML source. The information from web pages can be extracted from the source of a web page by tracking the appropriate HTML tags, keywords, images, URLs, and the associated text. Some natural language processing and machine learning techniques are applied to the extraction process from the textual description (e.g., price, email, and telephone). As mentioned before, there are techniques as named entity recognition (Mohit 2014), web information extraction systems (Chang et al. 2006), and text mining techniques (Vijayarani et al. 2015).

2.3 Knowledge Hosting

In our context knowledge is represented in the form of semantically enriched data. Semantically enriched means that metadata is added to describe the data (annotation of data), by using a standard (or de facto standard) vocabulary, according to the principles of RDF (Decker et al. 2000). In the current case, we use the schema.org[28] vocabulary, but the same methods also apply for other Ontologies. We discuss methods to populate, store, and retrieve data either from semantic annotations of web sites or directly from a Knowledge Graph.

---

[26]https://search.google.com/search-console/about

[27]https://support.google.com/webmasters/answer/9044175?hl=en&visit_
id=636862521420978682-2839371720&rd=1\#spammy-structured-markup

[28]https://schema.org/

2.3.1   Collection, Storage, and Retrieval of Semantic Annotations

Let us start with the collection, storage, and retrieval of semantic annotations.

Collection. Annotation collection can be established either by manual or semi-automatic editing, automatic annotation generation, or through mappings. For manual annotation, the SaaS annotation platform semantify.it provides an annotation editor with which annotations can be created via a form-like interface (see Sect. 2.2). Similarly, there also exist annotation plugins for WordPress and Typo3 that are called "semantify.it instant annotation" (see also the following paragraph on retrieval). If annotations already exist, they can be uploaded to the semantify.it platform via the upload functionality or through the API. If annotation should be automated, for big datasets based on classical data structures, then mappings can be defined, which are passed to the semantify.it wrapper. The wrapper then, periodically, translates the classical data sources according to the defined mapping.

Storage. To store semantically annotated data, a JSON-based document database works very well but comes with restrictions. A very convenient database for that purpose is the document store MongoDB. It is JSON based and hence supports JSON-LD (Sporny et al. 2014). Storing and retrieving data works, due to advanced indexing mechanisms, seamlessly, but reasoning over JSON-LD files inside a MongoDB[29] is not supported natively and requires extensive programming and processing power overhead. Even though MongoDB is not considered as a foundation for a Knowledge Graph, it still is a lightweight and cost-effective solution for storing a collection of schema.org-annotated information. We use it to store JSON-LD files of web annotations and replicate the data periodically or on demand into a graph database to populate the Knowledge Graph. Reasoning and data integration are solely done on the graph database. Data retrieval from MongoDB is done over an API. String- and index search is extremely performant, also on document stores containing several million JSON-LD files.

Retrieval. Annotations stored in semantify.it can be accessed directly through a shortened URL.[30] Requests sent to this URL, including the required parameter, respond with the pure JSON-LD file for the corresponding request. An example of such a query and its result can be found in Fig. 2.13. This request method was predominantly designed for on-the-fly integration of annotation files in websites. This means that when a specific website is loaded, it requests an annotation file and injects it into the website's source code on the fly. The server response time to retrieve annotations from semantify.it allows on the fly integration that works well with the general server response time of websites.

---

[29]https://www.mongodb.com/

[30]https://smtfy.it/

GET	{

https://smtfy.it/BJgn06IHNb	"@context": "http://schema.org",
	"@type": "LodgingBusiness",
	"name": "Haus Olmarausch",
	"disambiguatingDescription": "Unser Haus liegt in schöner, sonniger Lage inmitten von Leutasch. Wir bieten ein gut ausgestattetes heimeliges Haus und herzliche Gastfreundschaft. Wir wollen vor allem eines: Dass Sie sich von Anfang an wie zu Hause fühlen. \nDer Loipeneinstieg und befestigte Winterwanderwage sind direkt vis a vis vom Haus. \nIm Sommer Ausgangspunkt für herrliche Wanderungen und Radtouren auf schönen und sicheren Wander - und Radwegen in den Bergen von Leutasch. Das Ortszentrum, Gasthöfe und Bäckerei sind in kurzer Zeit erreichbar.",
	"@description": "<p>Unser Haus liegt in schöner, sonniger Lage inmitten von Leutasch. Wir bieten ein gut ausgestattetes heimeliges Haus und herzliche Gastfreundschaft. Wir wollen vor allem eines: Dass Sie sich von Anfang an wie zu Hause fühlen.
	Der Loipeneinstieg und befestigte Winterwanderwage sind direkt vis a vis vom Haus.
	Im Sommer Ausgangspunkt für herrliche Wanderungen und Radtouren auf schönen und sicheren Wander - und Radwegen in den Bergen von Leutasch. Das Ortszentrum, Gasthöfe und Bäckerei sind in kurzer Zeit erreichbar.</p>",
	"url": "https://www.tirol.at/urlaub-buchen/ferienwohnungen/a-haus-olmarausch",
	"image": {
	        "@type": "ImageObject",
	"name": "https://resc.deskline.net/images/SEE/1/472d237a-c4e5-470e-a8d3-51be428bb746/99/image.jpg",
	"contentUrl": "https://resc.deskline.net/images/SEE/1/472d237a-c4e5-470e-a8d3-51be428bb746/99/image.jpg",
	"url": "https://resc.deskline.net/images/SEE/1/472d237a-c4e5-470e-a8d3-51be428bb746/99/image.jpg",
	"uploadDate": "2017-01-01"
	},
	"address": {
	    "@type": "PostalAddress",
	},
	}

Fig. 2.13 The result of a query to semantify.it is a JSON-LD file

2.3.2   Collection, Storage, and Retrieval of Knowledge Graphs

Again, we discuss here collection, storing, and retrieval of facts, however, captured by a Knowledge Graph.

Collection. In order to collect and store data in the Knowledge Graph, there are two different possibilities in our framework:

1. Crawling: the semantify.it platform provides a crawling interface as part of the broker framework.[31] The broker crawler takes a list of URLs as input and crawls the websites and the corresponding web pages to a specific, predefined, depth. Semantic annotations are extracted and directly stored in a Knowledge Graph. Thereby, the serialization formats that should be considered (Microdata, RDFa, JSON-LD) can be defined, and schema.org classes to be ignored can be specified.
2. Mapping: the abovementioned semantify.it wrapper maps data sources to schema.org and stores it in the MongoDB database of semantify.it. Data produced by that wrapper can be exported to the Knowledge Graph. This functionality can either be called once or periodically or on demand—e.g., automatically whenever the dataset is changed.

The crawling of websites is a rather tedious task and can take up to hours or even days, depending on the size of the website, the depth of the crawl, and the number of websites given to the crawler. However, the average duration of transferring datasets (8 million facts per day in case of the touristic use case described in Sect. 2.5) to the Knowledge Graph is about 15 min.

Storage. Due to the RDF-nature of semantic data, a graph database is the most traditional way to store information in a Knowledge Graph. In order to store information in a Knowledge Graph, the aspects of data provenance, historical data, and data duplication have to be considered. In our touristic Knowledge Graph (TKG), historical data is kept in named graphs. To perform temporal reasoning, the identifier regex functionality is mandatory. Our Knowledge Graph currently includes around 5 billion facts (see Sect. 2.5).[32] Centralizing the storage of a Knowledge Graph could be viewed as a violation of the Linked Open Data principle of decentralized hosting of various data sources that get integrated through a query at run time (Bizer et al. 2008). However, this is not scalable in realistic settings (Fernández et al. 2017). The graph database GraphDB hosts the Knowledge Graph we build.[33] GraphDB features a SPARQL API over which the data is stored in the

---

[31] https://broker.semantify.it

[32] It is stored inside a GraphDB installation (Version: GraphDB GRAPHDB_ENTERPRISE v8.4.1 +sha.9a7a246c). The GraphDB installation is hosted on a Dell PowerEdge R430 Server running Linux Ubuntu, 16.04.5 LTS with 128 GB RAM, 2 Intel Xeon E5-2640 v4 processors with 10 cores and 2.40 GHz each. The data is stored on four 1.6 TB SSD (6 Gbit/s) disks, running on a hardware RAID 10.

[33] http://graphdb.ontotext.com/

Fig. 2.14 SPARQL query
to retrieve names of ski
resorts

```
PREFIX schema: <http://schema.org/>
SELECT DISTINCT ?name ?url WHERE {
    ?s a schema:SkiResort;
    schema:name ?name;
    OPTIONAL {?s schema:url ?url}
}
LIMIT 100
```

graph (see Harris et al. 2013). Besides RDF, serialization formats such as Turtle[34] and JSON-LD also non-RDF formats like XML, CSV, and others can be converted into RDF and stored in GraphDB.[35]

Retrieval. Data retrieval from an RDF-based graph database works with SPARQL. The SPARQL API of GraphDB works effectively and supports the current SPARQL version 1.1 (Harris et al. 2013). SPARQL is an RDF query language that can be casually explained as "SQL for graph databases." SPARQL can retrieve and maintain data stored in RDF format. The query's triple pattern syntax is compatible with Turtle. If, for example, all names and URLs (if exists) of ski resorts in the graph should be retrieved, the query looks like the one in Fig. 2.14.

More information on RDF storage technology can be found in Ma et al. (2004), Angles and Gutiérrez (2005), Stegmaier et al. (2009), and Faye et al. (2012).

2.4 Knowledge Curation

Building and hosting a Knowledge Graph is one thing. Turning it into a useful resource for problem-solving requires additional effort. The overall *goal* of knowledge curation is to provide cost-sensitive methods to improve the quality of large Knowledge Graphs ensuring their usefulness for envisaged applications: "There are two main goals of Knowledge Graph refinement: (a) adding missing knowledge to the graph, i.e., *completion*, and (b) identifying wrong information in the graph, i.e., *error detection*" (Paulheim 2017). We slightly extend this definition operationally by separating a general knowledge assessment task that guides further the knowledge cleaning and enrichment tasks. In analogy to data curation,[36] we refer to this overall process as knowledge curation.

Figure 2.1 already defines it as a loop of knowledge assessment, cleaning, and enrichment. During the following, we will discuss these three tasks in more detail. Our assumptions are:

---

[34]https://www.w3.org/TR/turtle/

[35]See Angles and Gutiérrez (2008) for a survey on graph database models.

[36]https://en.wikipedia.org/wiki/Data_curation

- A large Knowledge Graph has already been constructed (see Sect. 2.2).
- A large Knowledge Graph is properly hosted by a knowledge repository (see Sect. 2.3).

We first define a very simple knowledge representation formalism aiming to formalize schema.org and to refine our discussions on the knowledge curation subtasks. We conclude this section with some necessary future steps.

2.4.1 A Maximal Simple Knowledge Representation Formalism

We define our representation formalism in sync with schema.org to further structure and refine the developed definitions of knowledge curation. We distinguish schema definitions (TBox) and assertional statements over this vocabulary (ABox). The TBox defines types and their hierarchy as well as properties with their domains and ranges.[37] The ABox adds assertions over this terminology. First, we define the TBox. We have:

- Two disjoint and finite sets of type and property names T and P.
- A finite number of type definitions isA (t_1,t_2) with t_1 and t_2 are elements of T. isA is reflexive and transitive.
- A finite number of property definitions:
- hasDomain (p,t) with p is an element of P and t an element of T.
- Range definition for a property p with p is an element of P, t_1 and t_2 are Elements of T. Already (Hayes 1981) sketched out both options[38]:

  - Simple definition: *Global* property definition (Hayes 2004): hasRange(p,t_2)
  - Refined definition: *Local* property definition (Kifer et al. 1995): hasRange(p, t_2) for domain t_1, short: hasLocalRange(p,t_1,t_2)

An ABox is based on:

- A countable set of instance identifiers I. i, i_1, and i_2 are elements of I.
- Instance assertions: isElementOf(i,t). isElementOf is a special property with built-in semantics. If isA (t_1,t_2) AND isElementOf (i,t_1) THEN isElementOf(i,t_2).

---

[37]For the moment, we ignore the sub-property mechanism of schema.org as it seems to be a cumbersome workaround of the global property assumption of RDF. See our definition of locally defined ranges for properties.

[38]"One technicality is worth mentioning. In KRL, the same slot-name can be used in different frames to mean different relations. For example, the age of a person is a number, but his age as an airline passenger (i.e. in the traveler frame) is one of {infant, child, adult}. We could not allow this conflation and would have to use different names for the different relations. It is an interesting exercise to extend the usual first-order syntax with a notion of name-scope in order to allow such pleasantries" (Hayes 1981). See also Patel-Schneider (2014).

- Property value assertions: $p(i_1, i_2)$.
- Equality assertions: $isSameAs(i_1, i_2)$. We allow another built-in property to express identity of instances. It is symmetric, reflexive, and transitive. Every statement remains true or false when replacing i_1 by i_2 (and vice versa).

For the three phases, knowledge assessment, cleaning, and enrichment, we assume that the TBox is the *golden standard* and it is the ABox that needs to be reworked. This may not always be true but would require a manual extension of schema.org as described in Sect. 2.2. A full-fledged definition of the semantics of schema.org is provided in Patel-Schneider (2014).[39]

2.4.2 Knowledge Assessment

Knowledge assessment describes and defines the process of assessing the quality of a Knowledge Graph. The goal is to measure the usefulness of a Knowledge Graph considering two major quality dimensions, namely, its correctness and completeness. In this section, we first provide a literature survey on data/knowledge assessment, which includes an extended list of categories and quality dimensions shown below. Then we identify error sources according to the *maximal simple Knowledge Representation Formalism* defined in Sect. 2.4.1 and introduce specific tasks to address knowledge assessment. Finally, we investigate relevant methods and tools.

2.4.2.1 Literature

The literature on data quality is overwhelmingly extensive, indicating that it is a complex problem. Various categories and dimensions have been developed to measure and improve the quality of data such as Wang (1998), Wang and Strong (1996), Wang et al. (2001), Pipino et al. (2002), Batini and Scannapieco (2006), Zaveri et al. (2016), and Färber et al. (2018):

1. *Accessibility* implies that data or part of it must be available and retrievable (Färber et al. 2018); must contain a license and must be interlinked, secure, and high performance (Zaveri et al. 2016); and must be up-to-date of the data for a particular use case or consumers (Wang and Strong 1996). It is usually measured in terms of availability of the server, SPARQL endpoint, structured data, a license of data reuse, interlinks, and secure and high-performance access. For instance, let us suppose that a user searches for an event in Innsbruck and the event search engine returns an error response like *404 not found,* which means the resource is unavailable. Therefore, it is not accessible (Zaveri et al. 2016).

---

[39]For a discussion on these types and property definition as inference rules or constraints, see De Bruijn et al. (2005) and Patel-Schneider and Horrocks (2006).

2. *Accuracy* (veracity) defines the reliability, correctness (Wang and Strong 1996) [syntactically and semantically (Färber et al. 2018)], and truthfulness of the data with regard to external objects. In other words, a value is syntactically accurate if it does not violate syntactic rules (Fürber and Hepp 2011) or conforms a specification (e.g., valid schema.org types and properties used) and the value is semantically correct, that is, the value represents the correct state of an object (Fürber and Hepp 2011). For instance, let us suppose a user is searching for an event, and the event has the following identifier: https://www.mayrhofen.at/en/events/details/event/zillertal-krapfen-food-festival/, which represents the Zillertal Krapfen Food Festival. If in a Knowledge Graph the same identifier represents another event, this implies semantic inaccuracy, since the data is inconsistent with the actual event.[40]

3. *Appropriate amount*, also considered as part of the *Relevancy* dimension (Zaveri et al. 2016), defines the quantity of data that is appropriate for a specific task or use case. This metric can be measured in terms of the number of triples, classes, instances, and properties contained in a dataset (Flemming 2011). As an example, let us suppose a user is searching for events in Munich; to answer this query, the events search engine must contain an appropriate amount of data to cover various kinds of events (e.g., concerts, seminars, charity events). Besides, the data might cover transportation, accommodations, etc., that can help the user in planning his or her travel.

4. *Believability*, also part of *Trustworthiness* (Färber et al. 2018), defines the degree to which the data is regarded as true, credible, correct, real, trustable, unbiased, and verifiable (Färber et al. 2018; Pipino et al. 2002; Wang and Strong 1996; Zaveri et al. 2016). Usually, it is measured by checking the trust values or credibility of the data source (Pipino et al. 2002), the use of trust Ontologies (Färber et al. 2018), and trust annotations (Dezani-Ciancaglini et al. 2012). In addition, it can also consider user-based ratings as a relevant metric (Mendes et al. 2012). For instance, let us suppose a user is searching for events in Vienna; the events search engine shows a list of events and some of the results are provided by a well-known company. The user may be more inclined to select the events shown by this company since it is well-known. Alternatively, ratings given by other users may affect his or her decision.

5. *Completeness* of data refers to the data in a Knowledge Graph being *complete* [schema and instance level (Fürber and Hepp 2011)] given a specific use case. For instance, it can be measured by comparing the total number of classes, properties, values, and interlinks (Zaveri et al. 2016) of a knowledge base in comparison to a gold standard knowledge base.[41] Let us suppose a user is searching for events in Innsbruck; the events search engine contains all kinds of events of Innsbruck, and these events were described properly using a

---

[40]Here the real world is assumed to be the website where the event is published. See Sect. 2.2.3.5.

[41]In this case, "users should assume a closed-world assumption where a gold standard dataset is available and can be used to compare against the converted dataset" (Zaveri et al. 2016).

standard vocabulary. If a dialog system can answer all the questions about the events in Innsbruck, we can say that for this specific use case, the Knowledge Graph is complete.

6. *Concise representation* refers to how compactly [schema and instance level (Mendes et al. 2012; Zaveri et al. 2016)] the data are represented (Wang and Strong 1996). For instance, we can compare the total number of unique properties and instances with the overall number of properties and instances present in the knowledge base (Mendes et al. 2012). Let us suppose a user is searching for an event called K*inderolympiade* and the events search engine shows two representations for K*inderolympiade* value using different properties in the same knowledge base, e.g., *eventName=Kinderolympiade* and *name=Kinderolympiade* which introduces redundancy.

7. *Consistent representation* is the dimension referring to the consistency in terms of format (Wang and Strong 1996), formal descriptions (Zaveri et al. 2016), and other data stored in the Knowledge Graph (Mendes et al. 2012). It can be measured by checking if data is compatible with previous data (Wang and Strong 1996), whether there are disjoint classes' violations (Färber et al. 2018) and wrong usage of classes and properties; see more (Zaveri et al. 2016). For instance, having two different social security numbers for a person can cause inconsistency.

8. *Cost-effectiveness* measures the total cost of collecting a proper amount of accurate data to support the desired usefulness (Wang and Strong 1996). For example, calculation of the cost per triple with regard to how crucial the data is for a specific use case.

9. *Ease of manipulation* (a sub-dimension of *Ease of operation*) (Wang and Strong 1996) refers to how easy it is to manipulate and apply the data to different tasks (Pipino et al. 2002). For instance, whether there is a complete and precise documentation for tasks such as modification, classification, and aggregation (Mahanti 2019). Let us suppose a company want to integrate data from different sources to power their applications. If there is not a documentation of the classes, properties, and instances provided by an external knowledge source, the integration process can be very tough. This harms the data quality in the ease of manipulation dimension.

10. *Ease of operation*, refers to how easily data can be joined, changed, updated, downloaded, uploaded, reproduced, integrated, and customized for a specific task or purpose. This dimension may be also covered by the *Ease of manipulation* dimension (Wang and Strong 1996).[42]

11. *Ease of understanding* refers to how easy it is for humans to understand the data (Färber et al. 2018), clear and without ambiguity (Wang and Strong 1996). This

---

[42]It was described in Wang and Strong (1996) but then eliminated. This dimension is no longer considered in the following papers (Färber et al. 2018; Pipino et al. 2002; Zaveri et al. 2016) for the field of data quality.

quality dimension is covered by *Understandability* dimension (Zaveri et al. 2016; Färber et al. 2018).

12. *Flexibility* refers to how flexible, adaptable, extendable, expandable, and easily applied to different tasks (Wang and Strong 1996). This dimension is highly related to ease of manipulation dimension.

13. *Free-of-error* also refers to accuracy (Wang and Strong 1996). It refers to the degree to which data is correct (Pipino et al. 2002). The correctness can be measured by counting the number of errors like wrong and missing instance assertions, and property value assertions divided by the total number of statements in a knowledge base. For instance, let us suppose a user searches for events in Innsbruck. The event search engine shows a list of events with missing information (e.g., the time or place is missing) and wrong information (e.g., the wrong name of a place or misspelling). Those are indications that the data is not free-of-errors.

14. *Interoperability* refers to the level of re-using well-known standards, Ontologies, or vocabularies to describe the resources in a Knowledge Graph (Zaveri et al. 2016), increasing their machine-readability (Färber et al. 2018). Using a vocabulary such as schema.org is good example for measures that can be taken to increase interoperability.

15. *Objectivity* is also considered as part of the *Trustworthiness* dimension (Zaveri et al. 2016; Färber et al. 2018). It is used to measure how unbiased, objective (Wang and Strong 1996), unprejudiced, and impartial (Pipino et al. 2002) is the data. As objectivity of a Knowledge Graph, it is measured by experts and it depends on the type of information and also depends on whether the information can be confirmed by independent sources or providers. Let us suppose a user is searching for events and she is paying attention to the reviews regarding the prices, the comfort of the place, and so on. However, it may happen that a sponsor of the event search engine is ranked higher in the list of results. Therefore, this could be an indication of bias.

16. *Relevancy* refers to the level of applicability (Pipino et al. 2002) and relevancy of the data given a specific task (Zaveri et al. 2016). Let us suppose a user is searching for an event. The event search engine shows a list of events, but not only them, also historical information about the cities where the events are taking place, which may not be highly relevant for the task at hand.

17. *Reputation* can be considered as a part of *Trustworthiness* dimension (Färber et al. 2018), "refers to the degree to which data is highly regarded in terms of its source or content" (Wang and Strong 1996). For instance, it can be measured considering user's reputation score, via a survey in a community or page ranks (Mendes et al. 2012). Let us suppose a user searches for events with the best price. The event search engine returns a list of events with prices and so on. However, it might happen at the backend that some data sources have conflicting prices for an event. In that case, the event search engine takes the values from the source with a higher reputation for showing it to the user.

18. *Security* is considered as part of the *Accessibility* dimension (Zaveri et al. 2016). It refers how is the access to data is restricted (Wang and Strong 1996) in order

to maintain its integrity and prevent its misuse (Zaveri et al. 2016). It can be measured by checking whether standard security and privacy protection measures have been applied. For instance, let us suppose a user is paying for attending an event. The event search engine must ensure a secure payment transaction since personal data is highly sensitive (Färber et al. 2018).

19. *Timeliness* (velocity) is measured in terms of the freshness of data for a specific task (Pipino et al. 2002; Wang and Strong 1996; Zaveri et al. 2016). It measures the freshness of dataset based on currency and volatility, where volatility is the time needs to be passed before the data is invalid and currency is the time passed between the time data was refreshed and the time the data is delivered to the user (Zaveri et al. 2016). Timeliness is an important dimension, for instance, in accommodation and flight services where the prices are dynamically determined.

20. *Traceability* is also considered as verifiability (Wang and Strong 1996) and as part of the *Trustworthiness* quality dimension (Färber et al. 2018). Traceability refers to the degree to "which data is well documented, verifiable, and easily attributed to a source" (Wang and Strong 1996). This dimension is highly related to provenance metadata. For instance, data has metadata of the source, of the changes made, etc. Let us suppose the event search engine crawls data from different knowledge sources and it receives incorrect information that is shown to the users. In this case, the event search engine needs to be able to attribute the information to a source for verifying its trustworthiness.

21. *Understandability*, also called ease of understanding (Färber et al. 2018), refers to how easy it is for a human to comprehend the data unambiguously (Färber et al. 2018; Zaveri et al. 2016). It might be checked by detecting whether human-readable metadata, labels for classes, properties, and entities are available in a dataset (Flemming 2011). For instance, let us suppose a user searches for an event in Innsbruck. The data should contain clear human-readable labels, say, for the event location. Using "Innsbruck" instead of "IBK" would be more beneficial in terms of understandability.

22. *Value-added* refers to "the extent to which data are beneficial and provide advantages from their use" (Wang and Strong 1996). That is, data adds value to your operations (Wang and Strong 1996). Also, value-added is considered as part of the *Completeness* quality dimension by Färber et al. (2018). One simple metric can be to compute the ratio between total number of operations not using the data and the total number of operations using it. Suppose a user searches for hiking trails in Innsbruck at 1000 m of elevation. If the knowledge base contains elevation information, the application can return a list of hiking trails around *Nordkette* mountain (which might increase the chances of booking). Otherwise, it may just return all hiking trails in Innsbruck. In this case, elevation information is value-added.

23. *Variety* refers to a number of different sources from which the data is obtained. Let us suppose a user searches for events in Innsbruck. The event search engine returns a list of events from a variety of event knowledge sources such as Eventbrite,[43] feratel,[44] or Outdooractive[45] and instead of using a single source.

A survey on data assessment and improvement is provided by Batini et al. (2009). The authors describe a comparative analysis of methodologies, strategies, and techniques regarding data quality dimensions. These dimensions are a way to capture the usefulness of the data for given and expected applications ["The concept of fitness for use is now widely adopted in the quality literature" (Wang and Strong 1996)]. For example, Färber et al. (2018) adopt some of these criteria to compare several Knowledge Graphs such as Freebase, OpenCyc, Wikidata, and YAGO. Furthermore, Zaveri et al. (2016) introduce a quality assessment methodology that systematically adopts measures of data quality for Knowledge Graphs.

Paulheim et al. (2019) identify subtasks such as specifying datasets and Knowledge Graphs, specifying the evaluation metrics, specifying the task for task-specific evaluations, and defining the setting in terms of intrinsic vs. task-based and automated vs. human-centric evaluation, as well as the need to keep the results reproducible. In conclusion, besides having various *dimensions*, we also have different *metrics* and *evaluation functions* that define a score for such a dimension and *procedures* used to compute the scoring values.

2.4.2.2 Task Types

The core mission of knowledge assessment is to provide an overview of the amount of wrong or missing assertions in a Knowledge Graph. Given our maximal simple Knowledge Representation Formalism, we can distinguish three error sources:

1. Instance assertions: isElementOf(i,t)
2. Property value assertions: $p(i_1,i_2)$
3. Equality assertions: isSameAs(i_1,i_2)

Considering the correctness (i.e., wrong assertions) and completeness (i.e., missing assertions) quality dimensions and the error sources above, we can define six tasks for knowledge assessment:

• Correctness:

   1. Identify the number of wrong instance assertions.
   2. Identify the number of wrong property value assertions.
   3. Identify the number of wrong equality assertions.

---

[43]https://www.eventbrite.com/

[44]https://www.feratel.com

[45]https://www.outdooractive.com/

- Completeness

    4. Identify the number of missing instance assertions.
    5. Identify the number of missing property value assertions.
    6. Identify the number of missing equality assertions.

Given the goal of knowledge curation, which is to provide cost-sensitive methods, a life-cycle-based, cost-ratio-driven approach to improve the usability of the Knowledge Graph has to be defined.

2.4.2.3 Methods and Tools

There are different methodologies and tools to assess Knowledge Graphs. In the following, we describe some of them that can help to define metrics which are used to analyze data quality assessment.

Methodologies such as the *Total Data Quality Management (TDQM)* (Wang 1998) and *Data Quality Assessment* (Pipino et al. 2002) allow identifying the important quality dimensions and their requirements from various perspectives. Those perspectives are, for example, suppliers, managers, consumers, and manufacturers. Other methodologies define quality metrics that allow a semi-automatic assessment based on data integrity constraints. Those are, for example, user-driven assessment (Zaveri et al. 2013), test-driven assessment (Kontokostas et al. 2014), and a manual assessment based on human expertise [crowdsourcing-driven assessment (Acosta et al. 2013)]. Besides that, there are quality assessment approaches which use statistical distribution for measuring the correctness of statements (Paulheim and Bizer 2014), SPARQL queries for the identification of functional dependency violations, and missing values (Fürber and Hepp 2010a, b).

Regarding tools, some of them are already mentioned in Zaveri et al. (2016) and Debattista et al. (2016a), and we will describe more tools here. WIQA (Web Information Quality Assessment Framework[46]) uses filtering policies to evaluate information quality (Bizer and Cygania 2009); SWIQA (Semantic Web Information Quality Assessment Framework) (Fürber and Hepp 2011) defines data quality rules and quality scores for identifying wrong data; and LINK-QA (Guéret et al. 2012) is a framework for assessing the quality of data using network metrics. For example, one way to confirm a correct isSameAs relation is to find closed chains of isSameAs relations between the linking resource and the resource linked, tackling Task 3. Sieve (Mendes et al. 2012) is a framework for flexibly expressing quality assessment methods as well as fusion methods. Validata[47] (Hansen et al. 2015) is an online tool for testing RDF data conformance against present schemas written in the ShEx[48] (Shape Expressions) language. Luzzu (A Quality Assessment

---

[46]http://wifo5-03.informatik.uni-mannheim.de/bizer/wiqa/

[47]https://www.w3.org/2015/03/ShExValidata/

[48]https://www.w3.org/2001/sw/wiki/ShEx

Table 2.1 Available scoring functions in Sieve

Scoring function	Example
TimeCloseness	Measures the distance from the input date (obtained from the input meta-data through a path expression) to the current (system) date. Dates outside the range (informed in number of days) receive value 0, and dates that are more recent receive values closer to 1.
Preference	Assigns decreasing, uniformly distributed, real values to each graph URI provided as a space-separated list.
SetMembership	Assigns 1 if the value of the indicator provided as input belongs to the set informed as parameter, 0 otherwise.
Threshold	Assigns 1 if the value of the indicator provided as input is higher than a threshold informed as parameter, 0 otherwise.
IntervalMembership	Assigns 1 if the value of the indicator provided as input is within the interval informed as parameter, 0 otherwise.

Framework for Linked Open Datasets) (Debattista et al. 2016a) implements around 30 data quality metrics based on the Dataset Quality Ontology (daQ[49]).

The tools and methodologies above differ in how they measure or define data quality metrics. In the following, we describe four approaches that help to define metrics and tackle the assessment of the tasks defined before.

Sieve[50] *for Data Quality Assessment* (Mendes et al. 2012) is a framework that consists of two modules: a Quality Assessment module and a Data Fusion module.[51] The Quality Assessment Module involves four elements:

1. *Data Quality Indicators* allow to define an aspect of a dataset that may demonstrate the suitability of it for the intended use. For example, meta-information about the creation of a dataset, information about the provider, or ratings provided by the consumers.
2. *Scoring Functions* define the assessment of the quality indicator based on its quality dimension. Scoring functions range from simple comparisons, over set functions, aggregation functions, to more sophisticated statistical functions, text-analysis, or network analysis methods. See Table 2.1 for a set of scoring functions.
3. *Assessment Metrics* calculate the assessment score based on indicators and scoring functions, for example, recency and reputation. The assessment metrics can be classified into three categories, such as content-, context-, and rating-based metrics.
4. *Aggregate Metrics* allow users to aggregate new metrics that can generate new assessment values. For example, apply average, sum, max, min, or threshold functions to a set of assessment metrics.

---

[49]http://purl.org/eis/vocab/daq

[50]http://sieve.wbsg.de/

[51]We will explain this Fusion module in the context of knowledge enrichment.

Table 2.2 Type distribution of property *dbpedia-owl:location* in DBpedia (Paulheim and Bizer 2013)

Type	Subject (%)	Object (%)
owl: Thing	100.0	88.6
dbpedia-owl: Place	69.8	87.6
dbpedia-owl: PopulatedPlace	0.0	84.7
dbpedia-owl: ArchitecturalStructure	50.7	0.0
dbpedia-owl: Settlement	0.0	50.6
dbpedia-owl: Building	34.0	0.0
dbpedia-owl: Organization	29.1	0.0
dbpedia-owl: City	0.0	24.2
. . .	. . .	. . .

Using Semantic Web Resources for Data Quality Management (Fürber and Hepp 2010b) proposes methods to handle data quality problems using SPARQL queries, which uses a knowledge base as a trusted reference. In the following, we describe the problems tackled by this approach:

1. *Missing literal values* define two types of missing values: (1) values that must not be missing at all, for example, an empty literal attached to a datatype property, and (2) values that must not be missing in specific contexts, for example, the absence of a particular datatype property for an instance.
2. *False literal values* refer to (1) imaginary values, (2) wrong values, (3) values that are syntactically wrong, and (4) outdated values.
3. *Functional dependency violations* appear if the dependent literal obtains a value outside of the correct set of values. For example, compare a set of properties and values of instances to identify which of them do not have an identical value combination as in the trusted knowledge base.

SDType[52] (Paulheim and Bizer 2013) proposes to focus on the statistical distribution of relations between instances to infer their types using weighted voting. For each relation in a dataset, there is a statistical distribution of types for the subject and object position of the relation. For example, the property location is used in 24,601 statements in DBpedia with the distribution shown in Table 2.2. Hence, given a statement (X, location, Y), SDType may infer (with a certain statistical precision) that X is a place and Y is a place with 69% and 87.6% of probability, respectively. Besides, SDType defines a weight for each property, which measures the deviation of that property from the a priori distribution of all types, i.e., the weights help to reduce the influence of general-purpose properties.

Resolving Range Violations (Lertvittayakumjorn et al. 2017) proposes an approach that is based on reducing the search space and score methods for resolving range violation errors in a Knowledge Graph:

---

[52]Statistical Distribution of Type (SDType).

1. *Reduce search space* allows reducing the search space of all entities with the type of the range's property to only the entities related to the erroneous triple t = (s, p, o). It generates a set of candidate objects based on (1) all entities that are linked to the subject (s), (2) entities whose abstract contains any keyword generated from the object (o), and (3) entities that are linked to the object (o).
2. *Calculating scores* allows evaluating the likelihood that a candidate object is the correct one for the triple t. For that, the authors propose two methods: (1) Graph Method, which considers that the correct object has direct links, and (2) Keyword Method, which considers that keywords generated from the object (o) are in the abstract of the candidate object and they begin with a capital letter. Finally, it ranks all candidate objects.

The approaches mentioned above can cover one or various tasks defined in Sect. 2.4.2.2. For example, Paulheim and Bizer (2013) can be used to tackle the identification of missing instance assertions (i.e., Task 4), Fürber and Hepp (2010b) can identify wrong and missing type and property value assertions (i.e., Tasks 2 and 5), and Lertvittayakumjorn et al. (2017) can address the identification of wrong property value assertions (i.e., Task 2). The approach presented by Mendes et al. (2012) defines a few quality assessment metrics, which are not enough to tackle the tasks mentioned in Sect. 2.4.2.2. However, this approach can be adopted for defining more quality metrics for knowledge assessment.

2.4.3   Knowledge Cleaning

The *goal* of knowledge cleaning is to improve the correctness of a Knowledge Graph. This includes two major objectives:

- Identifying wrong assertions in a Knowledge Graph (*error detection*)
- Correcting wrong assertions (*error correction*) by deleting or modifying them

In order to achieve these objectives, assertions can be added to the Knowledge Graph, deleted, or modified. For evaluating the correctness of a statement, we have to again distinguish between verification and validation (see also Sect. 2.2.3.5 on evaluating semantic annotations). Verification is the process of evaluating the Knowledge Graph with a formal specification of integrity constraints; see Garcia-Molina et al. (2009). For example, we may require a unique value for a property like birthdate, name, or an identifier in addition to the standard requirements defined by schema.org. Also, we need to validate the Knowledge Graph that should accurately describe a domain. That is, we validate the correspondence of the Knowledge Graph with the so-called real world, whereas, for semantic annotations, we just had to validate against the virtual world of human-readable web content.

In the following, we provide a short survey of the literature, define the tasks included in knowledge cleaning, introduce a set of methods and tools applicable to them, and finalize with a summary and open research question.

2.4.3.1 Literature

In order to provide high-quality data, we need to ensure the correctness of a Knowledge Graph [i.e., free-of-errors (Pipino et al. 2002)]. The literature (Batini and Scannapieco 2006; Paulheim 2017, 2018a; Zaveri et al. 2016) presents approaches focused on the error detection or correction. However, it is difficult to find an approach suitable for both tasks. For example, once an error is detected, the erroneous assertion(s) will be removed, and a correction algorithm will try to find a proper instance or property value assertion. In addition to the literature review, we also observe that DBpedia is most frequently used for evaluation, which, in many cases, limits the significance of the result for domain-specific use cases.

That being said, it is relevant to make a careful analysis of errors, identification, and correction of them. Therefore, given our knowledge representation formalism, we can distinguish and enumerate all possible error sources in a Knowledge Graph. We present here the relevant literature for each error source, which includes wrong instance assertions (Esteves et al. 2018; Gangemi et al. 2012; Paulheim and Bizer 2013, 2014; Nuzzolese et al. 2012; Liang et al. 2017; Sleeman and Finin 2013), wrong property value assertions (Debattista et al. 2016b; Lertvittayakumjorn et al. 2017; Melo and Paulheim 2017), and wrong equality assertions (Esteves et al. 2018; Raad et al. 2018; Pernelle et al. 2018).

We observed that most of the approaches are focused on detecting errors than correcting them. Additionally, only a few approaches were accompanied by an implemented tool, and none of the existing tools covered all of our defined tasks (see the following subsection). The best coverage in terms of detection of errors was achieved by SDType (Paulheim and Bizer 2013) and SDValidate[53] (Paulheim and Bizer 2014), which exploit statistical distribution of types and relations to detect erroneous instance and property value assertions. In terms of correction of errors, we have found Katara[54] (Chu et al. 2015) for correcting wrong instance and property value assertions, HoloClean[55] (Rekatsinas et al. 2017) for correcting wrong property value assertions, and LOD Laundromat[56] (Beek et al. 2014) for syntax errors.

2.4.3.2 Task Types

Given our simple knowledge representation formalism, we try to *detect* the following *errors* in our set of assertions:

1. Detection of wrong instance assertions: isElementOf(i,t):

   – i is not a proper instance identifier.

---

[53]https://github.com/HeikoPaulheim/sd-type-validate

[54]http://da.qcri.org/ntang/dcprojects/katara.html

[55]http://holoclean.io/

[56]http://lodlaundromat.org/

- t is not an existing type name.
- The instance assertion is (semantically) wrong.

2. Detection of wrong property value assertions: $p(i_1, i_2)$:

- p is not a proper property name.
- i_1 is not a proper instance identifier.
- i_1 is not in any domain of p.
- i_2 is not a proper instance identifier.
- i_2 is not in any range of p where i_1 is an element of a domain of p.
- The property assertion is (semantically) wrong.

3. Detection of wrong equality assertions: $isSameAs(i_1, i_2)$:

- i_1 is not a proper instance identifier.
- i_2 is not a proper instance identifier.
- The identity assertion is (semantically) wrong.

Our *error correction* approach has to deal with these error types:

4. Correction of wrong instance assertion: $isElementOf(i, t)$:

- i is not a proper instance identifier: Delete assertion or correct i.
- t is not an existing type name: Delete assertion or correct t.
- The instance assertion is (semantically) wrong: Delete assertion or find proper t.[57]

5. Correction of wrong property value assertions: $p(i_1, i_2)$:

- p is not a proper property name: Delete assertion or correct p.
- i_1 is not a proper instance identifier: Delete assertion or correct i_1.
- i_1 is not in any domain of p: Delete assertion or add assertion $isElementOf(i_1, t)$ with t a domain of p.
- i_2 is not a proper instance identifier: Delete assertion or correct i_2.
- i_2 is not in the range of p for where i_1 is an element of a domain of p[58]: Delete assertion or add a proper isElementOf assertion for i_1. Such an assertion adds a domain for which i_2 is an instance of the range of the property. Alternatively, it adds a proper isElementOf assertion for i_2 that turns it into an instance of a range of the property applied to a domain of p of which i_1 is an element.
- The property assertion is (semantically) wrong: delete assertion or correct it. In this case, you should most likely define proper i_2, or search for better p, or search for better i_1.

6. Correction of wrong equality assertions: $isSameAs(i_1, i_2)$:

- i_1 is not a proper instance identifier: Delete assertion or correct i_1.

---

[57]Finding a proper i would neither scale nor make sense.

[58]The informed reader may here recognize the implicit usage of the closed versus open world assumption.

   – i_2 is not a proper instance identifier: Delete assertion or correct i_2.
   – The identity assertion is (semantically) wrong: Delete assertion or replace it by a SKOS operator, which however does not come with operational semantics.[59]

Finding and correcting these errors until an acceptable quality has been reached requires manual, semi-automatic, and automatic tool support, which are sketched in the following.

2.4.3.3   Methods and Tools

There exist several methods and tools for knowledge cleaning. Firstly, we distinguish methods according to the cleaning target (e.g., instance assertion, property value assertion, and equality assertion). Afterward, we describe the tools available for knowledge correction.

- *Instance assertion.* There are methods for identifying or correcting wrong instance assertions that use a statistical distribution of types and properties (Paulheim and Bizer 2013), disjointness axioms (Ma et al. 2014), supervised machine learning and entity-type dictionaries (Sleeman and Finin 2013), and association rule mining (Hipp et al. 2000).
- *Property value assertion.* For identifying wrong property value assertions and correcting them, there are methods that use statistical distribution (Paulheim and Bizer 2014), Ontology reasoners (Ding et al. 2007), Wikipedia pages (Lange et al. 2010; Muñoz et al. 2013), and outlier detection (Wienand and Paulheim 2014; Fleischhacker et al. 2014).
- *Equality assertion.* Wrong equality assertions can be addressed using methods such as outlier detection (Paulheim 2014), constraints (De Melo 2013), logical verification (Papaleo et al. 2014), and local context of instances (Raad et al. 2017).

Tools for knowledge cleaning can be built using different approaches. They utilize statistical distributions like SDValidate and SDtype, inferencing rules like SWIQA, constraints language like SPIN,[60] parsers like LOD Laundromat, statistical distributions and a constraint language like HoloClean, or external knowledge bases like KATARA. In the following, we give an overview of existing tools that cover various tasks related to identifying or correcting wrong assertions.

HoloClean (Rekatsinas et al. 2017) uses various approaches such as integrity constraints, external data, and quantitative statistics to detect errors. The HoloClean's workflow follows three steps: First, HoloClean takes a dataset, along with a set of methods and resources (such as denial constraints,[61] outlier detection,

---

[59]https://www.w3.org/TR/skos-reference/

[60]http://spinrdf.org/

[61]"Denial constraints are a generalization of many other integrity constraints widely used in databases," http://www.vldb.org/pvldb/vol11/p311-bleifub.pdf

external dictionaries, or labeled data) for detecting erroneous data. It splits input datasets into a noisy and clean dataset. Second, HoloClean assigns an uncertainty score over the value of noisy datasets, which is based on a probabilistic model generated using DDlog program.[62] Third, HoloCLean computes a marginal probability for each value to be repaired.

KATARA (Chu et al. 2015) identifies correct and incorrect data and generates possible corrections for wrong data. KATARA's process involves three steps. First, KATARA allows the user to select the target data table and the trusted knowledge base. Second, KATARA identifies the pattern (coherence of types and relationships) of the target data in the trusted knowledge base, and the user validates the pattern. Third, KATARA annotates each value and tuple (pair of values) as correct if they have the type and relations in the trusted knowledge base, respectively, otherwise as incorrect.

SDValidate (Paulheim and Bizer 2014) uses statistical distributions to assess (assigning a confidence score to) the correctness of statements. It involves three main steps: First, it computes the relative predicate (predicate/object combination) frequency for each statement. For example, statements with a low frequency are selected for a detailed analysis. Second, for each statement selected in the first step, SDValidate uses the statistical distributions of properties and types (predicate's subject/object combination) to assign a score of confidence to each statement. Third, SDValidate applies a threshold of confidence above which statements are considered to be true. Similarly, there exist SDType (which we have described in Sect. 2.4.2.3) which applies statistical distributions for detecting type assertion errors.

SPIN (SPARQL Inferencing Notation) is a SPARQL-based constraint language.[63] SPIN generates SPARQL Query templates based on data quality problems such as inconsistency, lack of comprehensibility, heterogeneity, and redundancy on the Semantic Web (Fürber and Hepp 2010a). For example, missing datatype properties, functional dependency violations, mistyping errors, and unique value violation (Fürber and Hepp 2010b). Nowadays, SPIN has turned into SHACL,[64] a language for validating RDF graphs.

The LOD Laundromat (Beek et al. 2014) is a platform that cleans Linked Open Data. LOD Laundromat takes a SPARQL endpoint or archived data as entry dataset, tries to guess the serialization format (for archived data), identifies syntax errors using a library[65] while parsing RDF, and saves RDF data in a canonical format.

---

[62]DDlog is a higher-level language for writing DeepDive applications and a DDlog program is a collection of declarations and rules. http://deepdive.stanford.edu/writing-dataflow-ddlog

[63]SPIN in Five Slides. https://www.slideshare.net/HolgerKnublauch/spin-in-five-slides

[64]Shapes Constraint Language (SHACL) is an official W3C recommendation. https://www.w3.org/TR/shacl/

[65]For identifying syntax errors LOD Laundromat uses the SWI-Prolog Semantic Web Library.

TISCO[66] (*Temporal Scoping of Facts*) (Rula et al. 2019) aims to determine the temporal scope of facts (i.e., the time intervals in which the fact is valid). TISCO follows three steps.

1. *Temporal evidence extraction* extracts information for a given fact from the web and DBpedia. For achieving the extraction, TISCO uses the DeFacto framework,[67] which returns possible evidence for a given fact. Then TISCO returns a list of all dates and their number of occurrences for a given fact.
2. *Matching* applies a local and global approach for normalizing the time scope. Local normalization takes the relative frequency of a fact, and global normalization considers the frequency of all facts that share the same subject. The Matching function returns interval-to-fact significance matrix associated with a fact (i.e., a fact associated with several time intervals).
3. *Selection and Reasoning* select the time intervals associated with a fact. Once there is a set of significance matrices, TISCO applies two functions. (1) *Neighbour-x* function selects the neighborhood of the time interval with the maximum significance score. (2) *Top-k* function selects intervals whose significance is close enough to the most significant interval. Finally, TISCO uses Allen's interval algebra[68] to merge two-time intervals associated with a fact.

The tools mentioned above cover our defined tasks partially. For example, SDType detects wrong instance assertions (Task 1), SPIN identifies functional dependencies violations (part of Task 2), LOD Laundromat allows the detection and correction of syntax errors (part of Tasks 2 and 5). SDValidate partially identifies wrong property value assertions (part of Task 2), KATARA identifies and corrects wrong property value assertions (part of Tasks 2 and 5), and HoloClean can be used for detecting and correcting wrong property value assertions (part of Tasks 2 and 5).

2.4.3.4   Summary

We have presented a literature review, defined tasks for addressing Knowledge Graph cleaning. Additionally, we have described approaches, methods, and tools error detection and correction. We consider the correctness quality dimension, and we concentrate on addressing the six tasks described in Sect. 2.4.3.2 that allows us to calculate the correctness of a Knowledge Graph.

Finally, we have observed that there is still a need for proper tools and methods that can handle the cleaning of Knowledge Graphs. We assume that knowledge verification and validation will become even more important since none of the methods and tools mentioned above can cover all the defined tasks.

---

[66]TISCO: http://tisco.disco.unimib.it/temporal-interval-scoping/

[67]DeFacto: http://aksw.org/Projects/DeFacto.html

[68]Allen's interval algebra: https://en.wikipedia.org/wiki/Allen%27s_interval_algebra

2.4.4 Knowledge Enrichment

The *goal* of knowledge enrichment is to improve the completeness of a Knowledge Graph by adding new statements. The process of knowledge enrichment starts with the identification of new relevant knowledge sources. However, discovering new sources is not always a straightforward task. For instance, the fact that large technology companies have launched their efforts to organize knowledge (Dong and Srivastava 2015) implies internal and external heterogeneity and overlap of information. For open sources, the increasing size of LOD cloud[69] has brought challenges in identifying relevant knowledge sources. Thus, it is a challenging task to identify the potential knowledge source for a specific task or domain (Lalithsena et al. 2013; Gunaratna et al. 2014). In our touristic use cases, alongside open sources, we are focused on proprietary knowledge sources, e.g., feratel,[70] intermaps,[71] Outdooractive,[72] and more. They need a manual process of identifying and accessing their knowledge sources as well as a legal negotiation process. Therefore, the possibility to mechanize such a process is quite limited.

Once we identify a relevant knowledge source, we start with the integration of TBox and ABox statements from that source to our Knowledge Graph. In that sense, Bleiholder and Naumann (2009) have identified the following three issues related to this:

Regarding the integration of TBox:

Issue 1. Merging or aligning different schemata

Regarding the integration of ABox:

Issue 2. Identifying (lack of isSameAs statements) and resolving duplicates
Issue 3. Invalid property statements such as domain/range violations and having multiple values for a unique property (also known in the data quality literature as contradicting or uncertain attribute value resolution)

Since we assume that we have mapped all potential data sources to schema.org (see Sect. 2.2), we will skip this first issue.[73] That is, we will focus on issues 2 and 3 (also described in Sect. 2.4.4.2). In the following, we provide a literature survey on knowledge enrichment, introduce specific tasks in our context, investigate relevant methods and tools for tackling these issues, and provide a wrap-up and outlook at the end of this section.

---

[69]https://lod-cloud.net/. See also West et al. (2014) as an approach for automated knowledge completion.

[70]http://www.feratel.at/en/

[71]https://www.intermaps.com/en/

[72]https://www.outdooractive.com/

[73]See, e.g., Batini et al. (1986).

2.4.4.1   Literature

Knowledge is a valuable asset (Wang 1998; Wang and Strong 1996; Pipino et al. 2002) in all enterprises. It is continuously gathered and maintained in order to serve several purposes, providing a common unified view on all data resources of the enterprises to power their applications. For instance, large technology companies have invested in knowledge source curation with the purpose of improving all their web-scale services (Pan et al. 2017b). In this context, a fundamental problem is the discovery of relevant knowledge sources for a given task since their knowledge sources are heterogeneous, incomplete, and have overlapping of information between each other. For addressing that, methods that use an artificial neural network model and Ontology matching (Rubiolo et al. 2009; Stegmayer et al. 2007) and tools like SEMINT (Li and Clifton 2000) have been proposed.

We can state that knowledge management shares some goals with data management[74]: data access, data quality, data cleansing, data integration, and more. At least, it faces many challenges that the data management community has been facing for decades (Wang 1998; Wang and Strong 1996; Pipino et al. 2002; Batini and Scannapieco 2006). Thus, when we talk about knowledge enrichment, we may also refer to Data Fusion. "Data fusion is the process of integrating multiple data sources to produce more consistent, accurate, and useful information than that provided by any individual data source."[75] That being said, and in order to produce more consistent, accurate, and useful knowledge, we must especially tackle the following issues:

- *Entity resolution*: Deriving new isSameAs(instance$_1$, instance$_2$) (Halpin et al. 2010) assertions and aligning the descriptions of these two identifiers [i.e., their property assertions; see Batini and Scannapieco (2006), Sect. 5, Bhattacharya and Getoor (2007), Christophides et al. (2015), Getoor and Machanavajjhala (2012), Paulheim (2017, 2018a)].
- *Resolving conflicting property value assertion*: Handling for example situations such as P(i$_1$, i$_2$), and P(i$_1$, i$_3$), and i$_2$ =/= i$_3$, and P has a unique value constraint; see Batini and Scannapieco (2006), Sect. 6, Dong et al. (2014b), Dong and Naumann (2009), Dong and Srivastava (2015), Paulheim (2017), and Paulheim (2018a). This refers to error detection and correction.

---

[74]https://en.wikipedia.org/wiki/Data_management

[75]https://en.wikipedia.org/wiki/Data_fusion

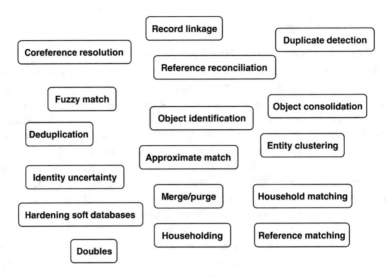

Fig. 2.15 Multiple names for a hard problem; see Getoor and Machanavajjhala (2012)

Author-name disambiguation,[76] Data Deduplication,[77] Entity Linking,[78] Identity Resolution,[79] Record Linkage,[80] Schema Matching,[81] and Single-instance storage[82] are different conceptual frames for a problem that is as old as computer science. For example, Record Linkage can be traced back to a publication from 1946 (Dunn 1946), finding out that (syntactical) different identifiers refer to the same entity; see Fig. 2.15. This name confusion is a solid indication that we talk about a real and hard problem that is not just an artifact constructed by the specific view of a single scientific community.[83]

---

[76]https://en.wikipedia.org/wiki/Author_name_disambiguation

[77]https://en.wikipedia.org/wiki/Data_deduplication

[78]https://en.wikipedia.org/wiki/Entity_linking

[79]https://en.wikipedia.org/wiki/Record_linkage#Identity_resolution

[80]https://en.wikipedia.org/wiki/Record_linkage

[81]https://en.wikipedia.org/wiki/Schema_matching

[82]https://en.wikipedia.org/wiki/Single-instance_storage

[83]"While entity disambiguation and resolution is an active research area in the Semantic Web, and now in Knowledge Graphs for several years, it is almost surprising that it continues to be one of the top challenges in the industry almost across the board. In its simplest form, the challenge is in assigning a unique normalized identity and a type to an utterance or a mention of an entity" (Noy et al. 2019). No, it is obviously not a surprise looking at the principal problems around equality; see Halpin et al. (2010).

2.4.4.2 Task Types

The goal of knowledge enrichment is to improve the completeness of a Knowledge Graph. For achieving this goal, we will define two tasks:

1. Identifying and resolving duplicates (lack of isSameAs(i_1, i_2) assertions).
2. Resolving conflicting property value assertions.

These tasks are solved by adding new statements to the Knowledge Graph. Given the *maximal simple Knowledge Representation Formalism* in Sect. 2.4.1, we try to add or delete the following assertions:

- Addition of missing instance assertions: isElementOf(i,t)
- Addition or deletion of property value assertions: $p(i_1,i_2)$
- Addition of missing equality assertions: isSameAs(i_1,i_2)

Identifying and resolving such assertions to reach a reasonable coverage requires manual, semi-automatic, and automatic tool support, which are sketched in the following.

2.4.4.3 Methods and Tools

Several methods and tools have been developed to address the tasks described above (i.e., identifying and resolving duplicates and resolving conflicting property value assertions). The resolution of duplicates may cause some property value conflicts that have to be resolved. In the following, we will describe (1) methods for identifying duplicates, (2) methods and tools for resolving duplicates, and (3) methods and tools for resolving conflicting property value assertions.

1. *Methods for identifying duplicates*

The identification of duplicates in Knowledge Graphs is a challenging task. To tackle it, some authors use methods and techniques based on string similarity measures (Winkler 2006), association rule mining (Hipp et al. 2000), topic modeling (Sleeman et al. 2015), Support Vector Machine (Sleeman and Finin 2013), property-based (Hogan et al. 2007), crowd-sourced data (Getoor and Machanavajjhala 2013), and graph-oriented techniques (Korula and Lattanzi 2014). Additionally, there are approaches aiming for the identification of duplicates for particular domains. For example, university data sources (Glaser et al. 2009), music datasets (Raimond et al. 2008), different DBpedia language editions (Aprosio et al. 2013), data sources that contain geospatial data (Giannopoulos et al. 2014), or social media platforms (Campbell et al. 2016). Besides, there are approaches focused on formalizing entity resolution, such as (Benjelloun et al. 2009) that define four properties (i.e.,

Idempotence,[84] Commutativity,[85] Associativity,[86] and Representativity[87]) for help-ing algorithms to address entity resolution.[88]

2. *Methods and tools for identifying and resolving duplicates*

Entity resolution has become an important discipline in different fields; thus, several methods and tools have been developed to address it and its related problems. In the following, we will describe some tools that help to address this issue.

- *ADEL* (Adaptable Entity Linking) (Plu et al. (2017)) aims to identify entities of texts and generate links [i.e., isSameAs(i_1,i_2)] to external knowledge sources for the identified entities. ADEL proposes a method for indexing and linking data based on the label and popularity of entities and it has a configuration as follows: (1) *Extractor* extracts likely entities from text based on different extractors (see Plu et al. 2017). (2) *Indexing* defines feature properties for entities to be indexed, e.g., id, a label, and a score. (3) *Entity Linking* generates a list of entity candidates for each extracted entity and defines the linking method, e.g., Levenshtein distance.[89]

- *Dedupe*[90] is a Python library that uses machine learning to find duplicate entries in a dataset. Dedupe may be used in two cases: (1) to identify duplicates in a dataset and (2) to find matches between two datasets. For the first case, dedupe takes a messy CSV[91] input dataset and a training examples dataset (entered by the user). For the second case, Dedupe takes two datasets with their field names and labeled training examples. The training examples are the core of Dedupe. The output of matching is added to the input dataset with an additional column that refers to the cluster IDs that Dedupe assigns to the grouped entities.

- *Duke*[92] (Garshol and Borge 2013) is a tool for identifying duplicated entities inside and across different sources. First, Duke loads a data source, e.g., CSV, JDBC, SPARQL, NTriples, and JSON. Second, it calls a cleaner that applies: string cleaners (LowerCase, DigitsOnly, and Trim), configurable cleaners (Regexp, MappingFile, and Parsing), as well as parsing cleaners (PhoneNumber, PersonName, Address, CompanyName). Third, Duke utilizes Lucene[93] for

---

[84]https://en.wikipedia.org/wiki/Idempotence

[85]https://en.wikipedia.org/wiki/Commutative_property

[86]https://en.wikipedia.org/wiki/Associative_property

[87]The meaning of the representativity property is that record r3 obtained from merging two records r1 and r2 "represents" the original records, in the sense that any record r4 that would have matched r1 (or r2 by commutativity) will also match r3 (Benjelloun et al. 2009).

[88]Some of the tools discussed during the following also cover duplication identification but are discussed in the broader context of enriched requirements.

[89]https://en.wikipedia.org/wiki/Levenshtein_distance

[90]https://github.com/dedupeio/dedupe

[91]https://en.wikipedia.org/wiki/Comma-separated_values

[92]https://github.com/larsga/Duke

[93]http://lucene.apache.org/

indexing data and finding potential matches. Fourth, Duke compares two string values and produce a similarity measure; it uses string comparators (Levenshtein, Jaro-Winkler, QGram[94]), simple comparators (Exact, Different), specialized comparators (Geoposition, Numeric, PersonName), as well as phonetic and token set comparators.

- *Legato*[95] (Achichi et al. 2017) is a linking tool based on indexing techniques. Legato implements the following steps: (1) Data cleaning that filters properties from two input datasets. For example, properties that do not help the comparison: "has_note" and "has_comment". (2) Instance profiling that creates instance profiles based on Concise Bounded Description[96] for the source. (3) Pre-matching that applies indexing techniques (it takes TF-IDF[97] values), filters such as tokenization[98] and stop-words removal, and cosine similarity to preselect the entity links. (4) Link repairing that validates each produced link against a target source.

- *LIMES*[99] (Ngomo and Auer 2011) is an approach for link discovery between a source dataset and a target dataset. LIMES comprises three steps: (1) Generation of a set of different examples for the target dataset, which represents a portion of a metric space.[100] (2) Calculation of the distance between each resource of the data source and each example. (3) Matching all instances of the data target where the approximation of the distance is less than the given threshold.

- *SERIMI* (Araújo et al. 2011) helps to match instances between two datasets. It has three steps: (1) property selection, allows the selection of relevant properties from the source dataset; (2) the selection of candidates from the target dataset, via string matching; and (3) the disambiguation of candidates, by measuring the similarity for each candidate applying Tversky's contrast model,[101] which returns a degree of confidence.

- *Silk*[102] (Volz et al. 2009) is a framework for achieving entity linking. Silk tackles three tasks: (1) link discovery that defines similarity metrics to calculate a total similarity value for a pair of entities (see Table 2.3), (2) evaluation of the correctness and completeness of generated links, and (3) a protocol for maintaining the data that allows source dataset and target dataset to exchange generated link sets. For instance, a protocol notifies a target dataset when the source dataset publishes a set of links pointing to the target dataset.

---

[94]https://github.com/larsga/Duke/wiki/Comparator#qgramcomparator

[95]https://github.com/DOREMUS-ANR/legato

[96]https://www.w3.org/Submission/CBD/

[97]https://en.wikipedia.org/wiki/Tf%E2%80%93idf

[98]https://en.wikipedia.org/wiki/Lexical_analysis#Tokenization

[99]http://aksw.org/Projects/LIMES.html

[100]https://en.wikipedia.org/wiki/Metric_space

[101]https://en.wikipedia.org/wiki/Tversky_index

[102]http://silkframework.org/

Table 2.3 Available similarity metrics in Silk

Similarity metric	Description
jaroSimilarity	String similarity based on Jaro distance metric[a]
jaroWinklerSimilarity	String similarity based on Jaro-Winkler metric[b]
qGramSimilarity	String similarity based on q-grams
stringEquality	Returns 1 when strings are equal, 0 otherwise
numSimilarity	Percentual numeric similarity
dateSimilarity	Similarity between two date values
uriEquality	Returns 1 if two URIs are equal, 0 otherwise
taxonomicSimilarity	Metric based on the taxonomic distance of two concepts
maxSimilarityInSet	Returns the highest encountered similarity of comparing a single item to all items in a set
setSimilarity	Similarity between two sets of items

[a]Jaro distance metric is a string metric measuring an edit distance between two sequences
[b]Jaro-Winkler Similarity is a variant of Jaro distance metric. https://en.wikipedia.org/wiki/Jaro%
E2%80%93Winkler_distance#Jaro%E2%80%93Winkler_Similarity

3. *Methods and tools for resolving conflicting property value assertions*

Entity resolution after integrating a new knowledge source into a Knowledge Graph is just the tip of the iceberg because the issues that come after are even bigger. For instance, once an equality assertion between two or more instances is added to a Knowledge Graph or when a new instance or property assertion is added, their property values may cause invalid property value assertions or conflicts with each other. Therefore, for resolving those conflicting property values, some authors have developed tools, which will be mentioned below.

- *FAGI*[103] (Giannopoulos et al. 2014) is a framework for fusing geospatial data, which has the following components: (1) *Transformation* normalizes the data in respect of the vocabularies used. (2) *Processing* indexes the data to produce similarity scores for fusion. (3) *Fusion* performs the fusion process using property mapping, calculation of similarity scores, and recommendation of fusion strategies. Furthermore, it suggests entity links or removal of existing links. (4) Finally, *Learning* trains machine learning models used for generating suggestion of fusion strategies.
- *FuSem* (Bleiholder et al. 2007) is a tool that implements five approaches to fuse conflicting values in a dataset. It utilizes different implementations of Outer Join[104] and Union SQL operations for combining two data sources. The authors also describe how to solve inconsistencies by grouping and to solve aggregation using FuseBy statement that proposes to extend the SQL syntax to support data fusion operation (Bleiholder and Naumann 2009). Besides, FuSem allows users

---

[103]https://github.com/GeoKnow/FAGI-gis

[104]https://en.wikipedia.org/wiki/Join_(SQL)#Outer_join

to postulate a set of key constraints together with their queries using ConQuer (Fuxman et al. 2005).

- *HumMer* (Bilke et al. 2005) is a tool that consists of four components: (1) A query language, HumMer uses Select-Project-Join[105] queries to sort, group, and aggregate data. For instance, it uses the column name of tables for identifying same properties across different tables. (2) Schema matching that uses an instance-based matching algorithm to detect duplicates between datasets and then gets attribute correspondences between them. For instance, it uses TF-IDF similarity.[106] (3) Duplicate detection that utilizes similarity measures such as edit distance[107] and some numerical distance functions[108] and then adds a new *objectID* column to the input dataset indicating the duplicated identifier. (4) Conflict resolution that resolves the conflicting values using strategies such as CHOOSE that returns the value provided by the specific data source or VOTE that returns the value that appears most often; see more (Bilke et al. 2005). Finally, the same objectID values are fused into a single tuple.

- *KnoFuss*[109] (Nikolov et al. 2008) provides data fusion using different methods. The overview of the workflow of KnoFuss is as follows: (1) It receives a dataset to be integrated into the target dataset; (2) it performs co-referencing using the Jaro-Winkler Similarity method, detects conflicts utilizing ontological constraints, and resolves inconsistencies using the Dempster-Shafer Theory;[110] as well as (3) it produces a dataset to be integrated into the target dataset.

- *ODCleanStore* (Knap et al. 2012) is a framework for cleaning, linking, quality assessment, and fusing of RDF data. The fusion module allows users to configure conflict resolution strategies based on provenance and quality metadata, e.g., (1) an arbitrary value, ANY, MIN, MAX, SHORTEST, or LONGEST is selected from the conflicting values; (2) computes AVG, MEDIAN, and CONCAT of conflicting values; (3) the value with the highest (BEST) aggregate quality is selected; (4) the value with the newest (LATEST) time is selected; and (5) ALL input values are preserved.

- *Sieve* (Mendes et al. 2012) is a framework that consists of two modules: a Quality assessment module (as explained in Sect. 2.4.2.3) and a Data Fusion module that is described below. The Data Fusion module describes various fusion policies that are applied for fusing conflicting values.

This Fusion module has the following elements:

---

[105] Select-Project-Join Expressions is a Relational Algebra expression it consists only of selections, projections and joins. http://mlwiki.org/index.php/Select-Project-Join_Expressions

[106] https://en.wikipedia.org/wiki/Vector_space_model#Example:_tf-idf_weights

[107] https://en.wikipedia.org/wiki/Edit_distance

[108] https://en.wikipedia.org/wiki/Distance

[109] http://technologies.kmi.open.ac.uk/knofuss/

[110] https://en.wikipedia.org/wiki/Dempster%E2%80%93Shafer_theory

Table 2.4 Available fusion functions in Sieve

Fusion function	Description
Filter	Removes all values for which the input quality assessment metric is below a given threshold
KeepSingleValueByQualityScore	Keeps only the value with the highest quality assessment
Average, max, min	Takes the average, chooses the maximum, or minimum of all input values for a given numeric property
First, last, random	Takes the first, last, or the element at some random position for a given property
PickMostFrequent	Selects the value that appears more frequently in the list of conflicting values

1. *Fusion* describes the name and description of a data fusion policy, e.g., name="Fusion strategy for DBpedia City Entities".
2. *Class* defines a subset of the input that belongs to a given class, e.g., Class name="dbpedia:City".
3. *Property* defines a property where a FusionFunction is applied, e.g., Property name="dbpedia:areaTotal"
4. *FusionFunction* specifies the *FusionFunction* class used to fuse for a given property (Table 2.4). For example, FusionFunction class="KeepValueWithHighestScore" metric="sieve:lastUpdated".

It is important to note that when we resolve property value conflicts from different sources, we need to know which data source is reliable. For instance, we can apply a voting strategy and consider giving a higher vote to a more trustworthy data source.

Truth-discovery techniques allow integrating noisy data by estimating the reliability of each source (Li et al. 2016). In the following, we will describe some approaches that have been proposed and used for truth-discovery:

- Kleinberg (1999) proposes an algorithm to discover "authoritative" pages, based on the relationship between a set of authorities and hub pages. Along the same line and trying to improve the proposed method, Borodin et al. (2005) have explored link analysis ranking algorithms for computing hub and authorities' weights, for example, Indegree,[111] PageRank,[112] Hits,[113] and the SALSA[114] algorithms. The authors propose new algorithms like Hub-Averaging, Authority Threshold, Max, and Breadth-First-Search, which modify Hits and Indegree algorithms for being applied on specific use cases.
- Dong et al. (2009a) proposes an approach that applies Bayesian analysis[115] to evaluate dependency between data sources and discover the truth-value from

---

[111] https://en.wikipedia.org/wiki/Directed_graph#Indegree_and_outdegree

[112] https://en.wikipedia.org/wiki/PageRank

[113] https://en.wikipedia.org/wiki/HITS_algorithm

[114] https://en.wikipedia.org/wiki/SALSA_algorithm

[115] https://en.wikipedia.org/wiki/Bayesian_inference

conflicting information. For conflicting data, they count the vote for a particular value considering the out-degree of the data in the data source. Then, for finding the true values, they propose an algorithm called VOTE that takes the value with the maximal vote count as the true value. In the same line, they utilize the Hidden Markov Model[116] for discovering copying sources.

- Wu and Marian (2007) proposes a method for ranking the query answers from different sources (e.g., websites). The ranking is based on the importance and similarity of the sources reporting each answer. For defining the importance of an answer, they (1) identify the answers; (2) aggregate a relevance score of similar answers considering the importance of the source, for example, the duplication of information and the prominence of the answer; and (3) corroborate the frequency of the answers in the set of sources.

- Menestrina et al. (2010) propose a distance measure for entity resolution called Generalized Merge Distance (GMD) based on edit distance, which is a common measure in other domains such as string-to-string matching. Besides, they propose an algorithm called Slice which computes GMD.

2.4.4.4 Summary

Knowledge enrichment is a hard and important task. The current literature has shown the existence of tools that help to tackle the issues regarding duplicate detection and for resolving conflicting property values. Thus, the addition of missing equality assertions can be resolved using ADEL, Duke, Dedupe, Legato, LIMES, SERIMI, and Silk, and the addition of missing instance and property assertions can be addressed using FAGI, FuSem, HumMer, KnoFuss, ODCleanStore, and Sieve. We have seen that most of the tools need a previous configuration to start working, such as Silk and Sieve. Also, most of the approaches focus on an individual type of use cases. For example, FAGI focuses on geospatial data.

Finally, we have noticed that there are still some open questions like how to scale efficiently an approach for a Knowledge Graph with billions or trillions of triples and how to represent effectively and efficiently the consolidated entities in an updated Knowledge Graph.

2.4.5 Summary on Knowledge Curation

Schema.org is a rather limited knowledge representation formalism. For example, we do not have integrity constraints. We cannot express that a property has a unique value for a certain property. However, such conflicting property values are a typical result when integrating multiple data sources for knowledge enrichment. We have

---

[116]https://en.wikipedia.org/wiki/Hidden_Markov_model

defined an extension of schema.org using the Shapes Constraint Language (SHACL)[117] to add such means to our simplistic knowledge representation formalism (see Appendix).

Also, the discussed truth value assignment to assertions is rather a simplistic false/true rather than a certain likelihood or a given context in which an assertion is evaluated to a certain truth value. Defining preferences, rankings, and probabilities provides a wide range of more useful but also significant more complex approaches for knowledge curation. Obviously, we have to prevent ourselves from entering the hyper complex area of *belief revision*[118] in all its variations.

In general, knowledge curation is still an emerging area of science and much more work need to be spent to develop appropriate methodologies, methods, and tools for it (Paritosh 2018).

2.5 Knowledge Deployment: The Use of the Pudding Is in the Eating

Here the topic of Linked Open Data (LOD) comes into play which is a means to publish data openly and according to some principles, based on semantic technologies, which allow the data to be easily reused due to the implicit machine read- and interpretability (Bizer et al. 2008). To introduce the term Linked Open Data, it is necessary first to explain the terms Open Data and Linked Data in separation, of which LOD consists. Open Data is, according to the Open Data Handbook,[119] "...data that can be freely used, re-used and redistributed by anyone—subject only, at most, to the requirement to attribute and share alike" (Dietrich et al. 2009). Linked data, according to the definition in Bizer et al. (2009), "is a method of publishing structured data so that it can be interlinked and become more useful through semantic queries." Linked Open Data is Linked Data published as Open Data or Open Data published as Linked Data. The quality of LOD can be measured by applying the 5* criteria according to Janowicz et al. (2014):

*) The dataset gets awarded one star if the data are provided under an open license.
**) Two stars if the data are available as structured data.
***) Three stars if the data are also available in a non-proprietary format.
****) Four stars if URIs are used so that the data can be referenced.
*****) Five stars if the dataset is linked to other datasets to provide context.

The LOD-cloud is a collection of LOD sets which all are published according to the five-star criteria. As of November 25, 2018, there are 1365 datasets in the cloud with more than 16,000 links describing fields like Geography, Life Science, Media,

---

[117]https://www.w3.org/TR/shacl/

[118]https://en.wikipedia.org/wiki/Belief_revision

[119]http://opendatahandbook.org

Social Networks, and more. To store LOD, Knowledge Graph (as mentioned above) is a suitable format. Typically, the data can be queried through a SPARQL endpoint (Harris et al. 2013).

We have built the Tirol Knowledge Graph (TKG) as a five-star linked open dataset published in a graph database providing a SPARQL endpoint (Kärle et al. 2018), for the provisioning of touristic data of Tyrol, Austria. The TKG currently contains data about touristic infrastructures, like accommodation businesses, restaurants, and points of interests, events, and recipes. The data of the TKG fall under three categories of data: Static data is information which is rarely changing, like addresses of hotels, descriptions of points of interests, and alike. Dynamic data is fast-changing information, like availabilities and prices. Active data describes actions that can be executed, for example, the description of purchase or reservation Web API that can be accessed through the TKG GraphDB platform[120] (see for more details Sects. 4.3 and 4.4).

The data are collected either through the crawling of websites or mappings from proprietary data sources into the Knowledge Graph that is using schema.org as Ontology. So only websites containing schema.org annotated data are considered and data sources are always mapped to schema.org before stored. The crawler is implemented inside the semantify.it annotation platform (Kärle et al. 2017), called broker.semantify.it. Based on a list of URLs of touristic websites, the data gets collected periodically and is then stored in the graph. The mapping is provided for different data sources such as Feratel,[121] General Solutions,[122] Infomax,[123] and Tomas[124] (Panasiuk et al. 2018b, c). The data is mostly retrieved through SOAP or REST APIs and are originally provided in XML or JSON format. For fetching these data, translating it to schema.org and storing it in the Knowledge Graph periodically, wrappers are implemented inside semantify.it that are executed periodically. The mapping is either implemented programmatically in NodeJS or done through the mapping language RML (Dimou et al. 2014).

On November 25, 2018, the TKG contained around 5 billion statements, of which 55% are explicit and 45% are inferred. Every day the Knowledge Graph grows by around 8 million statements. The data are held in around 2000 subgraphs, where every subgraph represents one import process per data source. TKG contains more than 200 entity types; the most frequently used ones are shown in Table 2.5.

To demonstrate the possibilities of the TKG and to evaluate its usability, we have built several pilots.

1. *Dialog-driven room booking:* Among the crawled websites, many are customers of the Internet booking engine provider Easybooking.[125] The features, identifying

---

[120]http://graphdb.sti2.at:8080/

[121]https://www.feratel.com/

[122]https://general-solutions.eu/php/portal.php

[123]https://www.infomax-online.de/

[124]https://www.tomas.travel/

[125]https://www.easybooking.eu/de/

Table 2.5 Top ten entities used in the TKG

Entity	Count
schema: Thing	453,841,147
schema: CreativeWork	175,787,490
schema: MediaObject	175,746,110
http://purl.org/dc/dcmitype/Image	175,735,868
schema: ImageObject	175,735,868
schema: Intangible	172,124,244
schema: StructuredValue	155,482,666
schema: Place	60,996,190
schema: ContactPoint	53,155,166
schema: PostalAddress	51,706,023

a website as customer of Easybooking, inside the source code are known. The booking API structure of Easybooking is known too. We developed an Alexa skill that enables voice-driven booking of Easybooking hotels through the TKG. If the showcase skill is asked for a certain hotel, it sends a request to a webhook. The result, a list of available hotel offers, is sent back to the skill and read to the user. The list also contains annotated API descriptions for the booking API. So, if the user decides on an offer, a booking can be executed through a voice command.

2. *Showcase dialog system:* as described in Şimşek and Fensel (2018b) and Panasiuk et al. (2018a), we built two dialog systems that fetch their data from the graph. One (Panasiuk et al. 2018a) answers generically to touristic topics like hiking or opening hours. The other one (Şimşek and Fensel 2018b) goes one step further and conducts generic dialogs solely based on data taken from the Knowledge Graph.

3. *Time series analysis of prices in touristic regions:* Since all the prices of offers, if available, are stored permanently, a time series analysis can be conducted. We compared the price development of two touristic regions over a while. Time series analysis work perfect with Knowledge Graphs and is a promising application of them in tourism.

TKG goes FAIR: FAIR[126] is an acronym and stands for findability, accessibility, interoperability, and reuse. FAIR was introduced in Wilkinson et al. (2016) and intended to provide principles to improve the machine-accessibility of published datasets. The TKG aims to follow those principles and improve their adoption continually, currently by taking the following measures:

– *Findability*: The data is identified uniquely and described with metadata following RDF principles.
– *Accessibility*: the data is accessible over a web UI, through HTTP, or a SPARQL API. Authentication or authorization is not required.

---

[126]https://www.go-fair.org/fair-principles/

```
PREFIX schema: <http://schema.org/>
SELECT DISTINCT ?name ?street ?location ?zip WHERE {
        ?s a schema:LodgingBusiness;
        schema:name ?name;
        schema:address ?address.
        ?address schema:addressLocality ?location;
        schema:streetAddress ?street;
        schema:postalCode ?zip.
FILTER (regex(str(?location), "Mayrhofen") || regex(str(?location),
"Ginzling") || regex(str(?location), "Ramsau") || regex(str(?loca-
tion),
"Schwendau") || regex(str(?location), "Hippach") ||
regex(str(?location), "Brandberg"))
}
```

Fig. 2.16 A SPARQL query retrieving all lodging businesses and their addresses in the Mayrhofen region

Table 2.6 A sample result set of a query returning all lodging businesses and their addresses in the Mayrhofen region from the Tirol Knowledge Graph

Name	Street	Location	Zip
Wechselberger Lukas	Hochschwendberg 678	Hippach	6283
Aschenwald Ingrid	Zillerlände 489	Mayrhofen	6290
Sieghard, Das kleine Hotel mit der großen Küche	Johann-Sponring-Straße 83	Schwendau/Hippach	6283
Haus Mauracher	Burgstall 346	Mayrhofen	6290
Veitlerhof	Schwendberg 322	Hippach	6283
Apartment Stock	Zillergrundweg 573	Mayrhofen	6290
...	...	...	...

- *Interoperability*: The language that is used to access the data is SPARQL, which is a W3C recommendation. The vocabulary to describe the data is schema.org, which is a de facto standard to describe data on the Web.
- *Reusable*: The data is available openly, the provenance is stated, and it meets the domain-relevant community standards which were created in cooperation with domain experts.

An example query from Tirol Knowledge Graph, retrieving all lodging businesses from the region of Mayrhofen, can be seen in Fig. 2.16.

The result of that query contains 1475 distinct lodging businesses; a sample output can be seen in Table 2.6.

Another query example from the Tirol Knowledge Graph returns all Restaurants in Seefeld (see Fig. 2.17).

```
PREFIX schema: <http://schema.org/>
SELECT DISTINCT ?name ?street ?location ?zip WHERE {
    ?s a schema:Restaurant;
      schema:name ?name;
      schema:address ?address.
    ?address schema:addressLocality ?location;
            schema:streetAddress ?street;
            schema:postalCode ?zip.
      FILTER regex(str(?location), "Seefeld")
    }
```

Fig. 2.17 A SPARQL query retrieving all restaurants and their addresses in Seefeld

Table 2.7 A sample result set of a query returning all restaurants and their addresses in Seefeld from the Tirol Knowledge Graph

Name	Street	Location	Zip
Hotel Hocheder	Klosterstr. 121	Seefeld	6100
Tiroler Weinstube	Dorfplatz 130	Seefeld	6100
Birkenlift Food and Drink, Restaurant	Leutascherstraße 634	Seefeld in Tirol	6100
Restaurant—Alt Seefeld	Olympiastr. 101	Seefeld	6100
Astoria Relax and Spa Hotel	Geigenbühelstr. 185	Seefeld	6100
Hirschen	Leithener-Dorf-Strasse 9	Reith bei Seefeld	6103

This query returns 324 distinct restaurants; a sample can be seen in Table 2.7.

Even though the Tirol Knowledge Graph (TKG) grows daily, it still suffers from many disconnected nodes. The reason for that is the heavy use of blank nodes due to the design of the schema.org vocabulary, instead of identifying things with URIs. A lot of web addresses, which could cater as URIs for things, are encoded as RDF literals instead of URIs. Therefore, as can be seen in the queries above, there are no URIs for regions like Mayrhofen or villages like Seefeld, and queries must use SPARQL filters to distinguish. This could only be tackled if either the data providers use proper URIs at the knowledge generation phase or via knowledge curation efforts. Finding proper URIs for such entities (e.g., http://dbpedia.org/resource/Seefeld_in_Tirol for Seefeld) and making the necessary property value assertions can be a good practice for knowledge enrichment.

The Tirol Knowledge Graph currently consists of Tyrolean data. However, geographical borders should not stop LOD endeavors. That is why we are about to join forces with touristic stakeholders to extend the reach and visibility of our Open Touristic Knowledge Graph to all the German-speaking parts of Italy and

Table 2.8 Numerical overview of some Knowledge Graphs, taken from Paulheim (2017)

Name	Instances	Facts	Types	Relations
DBpedia (English)	4,806,150	176,043,129	735	2813
YAGO	4,595,906	25,946,870	488,469	77
Freebase	49,947,845	3,041,722,635	26,507	37,781
Wikidata	15,602,060	65,993,797	23,157	1673
NELL	2,006,896	432,845	285	425
OpenCyc	118,499	2,413,894	45,153	18,526
Google's Knowledge Graph	570,000,000	18,000,000,000	1500	35,000
Google's Knowledge Vault	45,000,000	271,000,000	1100	4469
Yahoo! Knowledge Graph	3,443,743	1,391,054,990	250	800

See Noy et al. (2019) for more actual figures on Bing, eBay, Facebook, Google, and IBM. For example, for Google they report 70 billion assertions about 1 billion entities

Switzerland, as well as Austria and Germany.[127] The working group behind this initiative is called DACH-KG.[128] To reach the ambitious goal of a unified touristic Knowledge Graph for the German-speaking countries and beyond, the DACH-KG working group is also working on a unified vocabulary. The foundation for this vocabulary is schema.org. Beyond the expressivity of schema.org, DACH-KG develops extensions to that vocabulary. Those extensions will be more domain specific and more expressive, but still widely understandable, due to the close relation to schema.org.[129]

However, building, implementing, and curating Knowledge Graphs are time-consuming and costly activities. Integrating large amounts of facts from heterogeneous information sources does not come for free (Paulheim 2018b) and estimates the average cost for one fact in a Knowledge Graph between $0.1 and $6 depending on the amount of mechanization. Table 2.8 provides a survey on the size of some Knowledge Graphs where this information is made publicly available.

These costs must be covered. In principle, there are two alternatives for such a cost model:

- The data consumer is paying for this service. Accessing this data must have value for him.
- The data supplier is paying for this service. This is often called Open Data or Linked Open Data. Providing this data must have value for him.

Similarly, we can distinguish between proprietary and public Knowledge Graphs. For example, the Google Knowledge Graph is an internal resource of Google to improve its answering quality. Alternatively, a public Knowledge Graph can be the

---

[127]https://www.tourismuszukunft.de/2018/11/dach-kg-auf-dem-weg-zum-touristischen-knowledge-graph/

[128]https://www.tourismuszukunft.de/2018/11/dach-kg-auf-dem-weg-zum-touristischen-knowledge-graph/

[129]https://github.com/STIInnsbruck/dachkg-schema

basis of eco-systems of bots that search for products and services. Many variations and combinations of these two principles are possible.

Many people in academia prefer the open model; however, it is also clear that the investment costs must be backed up by a proper business model. Providing infrastructure for free disable the usage of costs as a resource allocation procedure, just as spam is a consequence of free email traffic, and as advertisement is the dominant business model on the web (Vardi 2018).

In conclusion, such an investment can only be justified with a purpose in mind. For a search engine like Google, it is used in search result improvement. Many business entities see the value in the information integration service that further facilities their business. In the following section, we develop an application layer on top of Knowledge Graphs that facilitate goal-oriented dialog-based access to data, content, and services. Obviously, this can turn such a Knowledge Graph into a powerful resource for e-marketing and e-commerce. Using Knowledge Graph technology in a commercial setting is further discussed in Chap. 4.

Chapter 3
How to Use a Knowledge Graph

Abstract Intelligent Personal Assistants are changing the way we access the information on the web as search engines changed it years ago. Undoubtfully, an important factor that enables this way of consuming the web is the schema.org annotations on websites. Those annotations are extracted and then consumed by search engines and Intelligent Personal Assistants to support tasks like question-answering. In this section we explain how Knowledge Graphs built based on content, data, and service annotations can improve search engine results and conversational systems. We first give a brief overview of the history of the Internet, AI, and web and the role semantic technologies is playing in bringing those three to the point we are today. Then we show the need for an abstraction layer over Knowledge Graphs where we can create different knowledge views in order to achieve scalable curation, reasoning, and access control. Finally, we show how Knowledge Graphs can power conversational agents in different points in the dialog system pipeline and the promising future of service annotations helping to build flexible systems decoupled from the web services with which they communicate.

3.1 Introduction

We are currently at the beginning of a significant paradigm shift in accessing and sharing information on the Internet. This is not the first time that the Internet has drastically changed the way we cooperate and communicate. With email arose (nearly) instant online communication and with the web a worldwide platform for information sharing. Both significantly altered the way marketing and commerce are done. Currently, we see a new access layer arising on top of them. Bots and Intelligent Personal Assistants access and aggregate information on behalf of human users. Humans no longer need to interact with lower levels such as the web but trust their favorite bots that they do this on their behalf. First, this requires that these bots understand human language, written or spoken. Second, the descriptions of available resources no longer need to be provided to human users directly but must be enriched by semantic annotations to provide machine processability and understandability by bots. Both require results from Artificial Intelligence such as

© Springer Nature Switzerland AG 2020
D. Fensel et al., *Knowledge Graphs*, https://doi.org/10.1007/978-3-030-37439-6_3

natural language processing and Semantic Web technology facilitating Knowledge Graphs. Building and maintaining Knowledge Graphs is a challenging effort. In this section, we focus on them as infrastructure for dialog-based information and service access. We first introduce the merger of AI and Internet technology as it currently has been happening in Sect. 3.2. Then we discuss in Sect. 3.3 how to access Knowledge Graphs and optimize the interaction with them. We introduce this architecture as a means for open dialog systems being able to not only answer questions but to guide a dialog based on semantically annotated content, data, and services, as shown in Sect. 3.4.[1]

3.2   Merging Artificial Intelligence and the Internet

Here we give a brief overview of the development of Artificial Intelligence and its application on the web of bots.

3.2.1   60 Years of AI in a Glimpse

Many researchers point to the proposal for the *Dartmouth Summer Research Project on Artificial Intelligence (AI)*[2] in 1956 as the starting point of research on AI. In its beginning, the optimism in achieving intelligent machines was overwhelming, given the actual theoretical and practical means that were around these days. The under-lying assumptions were simple:

- Logic expressions can define any problem (or solution).
- A solution can be found by applying a formal reasoning engine, a kind of theorem prover, to these logical statements.

This approach was also called the *General Problem Solver*[3] because it can be applied to any problem. However, such an approach did not deploy intelligence and therefore, did not provide scalable solutions. Logic reasoning is inherently complex (NP-hard to undecidable) because without any grounding knowledge, any (of potential infinite) possible reasoning traces must be explored.

In conclusion, the slogan "Knowledge is power"[4] was coined and started a new trace on research providing means for presenting knowledge formally to make it machine-understandable. A steady flow of knowledge representation formalisms

---

[1]Compare (Singh et al. 2018) that have the same aim but propose a tighter connection of the different tasks.

[2]http://www-formal.stanford.edu/jmc/history/dartmouth/dartmouth.html

[3]https://en.wikipedia.org/wiki/General_Problem_Solver

[4]By Feigenbaum and taken from Sir Francis Bacon.

was developed. The assumptions were that as more knowledge about the problem, its context, possible solutions, and variations of goals would be described as more efficient reasoning can be performed. This also reflects the meaning of the term "intelligence" in the English language. It does not only refer to an abstract reasoning ability but specific knowledge about a domain or task.

Unfortunately, what was meant as a solution just opened a new rabbit hole. Knowledge can only be formalized when it is available. The research fields of *knowledge acquisition* and *knowledge engineering* arose to provide methodological support for the challenge to build up such knowledge in a machine-processable manner.[5] These fields were aiming to describe the initial tasks associated with developing an expert system, namely, finding and interviewing domain experts and capturing their knowledge via workflows, rules, objects, and Ontologies. Unfortunately, a core insight of this research was the discovery of the so-called knowledge acquisition bottleneck:

- Acquiring, modeling, and representing this knowledge was an extremely costly endeavor.
- Most knowledge systems were small, shallow, not connected to overall processes in the enterprise, and not applicable to additional domains and tasks that steadily evolve.

Projects such as CYC[6] that were aiming at modeling the entire human common-sense knowledge just proved that modeling this human world knowledge is a non-feasible task. As a result, the final phase arose, the so-called AI winter, and working as a researcher in this field became quite an uncool experience in various aspects.

3.2.2 The Web (for Bots)

Let us jump into something "completely" different. The *Internet* started in the 1960s as a local network of four computers in the USA and evolved over the next 20 years into a worldwide computer network. An early paradigm shift for human communication based on it was *email*, which has provided an instant messaging service to a fast-growing number of people. A complementary interaction paradigm started in 1989 based on the work of Sir Tim. Instead of messaging, the *World Wide Web* (*WWW*) is based on publishing information to many potential readers. The web is an information space where documents and other web resources are described by hypertext markup, interlinked by hypertext links, identified by URIs, *and* can be

---

[5]See, for example, CommonKads which has been a leading approach in Europe on these topics. https://commonkads.org/

[6]https://en.wikipedia.org/wiki/Cyc

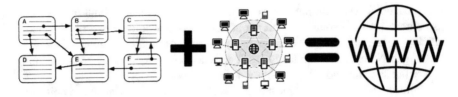

Fig. 3.1 The essence of the Web

Some Ontology Definitions

Concept Hierarchy	Attribute Definitions	Rules
Object[].	Person[	FORALL Person1, Publication1
Person::Object.	firstName =>> STRING;	Publication1:Publication
Employee::Person.	lastName =>> STRING;	[author ->> Person1]
AcademicStaff::Employee.	eMail =>> STRING;	<->
Researcher::AcademicStaff.	...	Person1:Person
Publication::Object.	publication =>> Publication].	[publication ->> Publication1].
	Employee[	
	affiliation =>> Organization;	
	...].	

```
<html>     <body>
           <a onto="page:Researcher">
           <h2>Welcome on my homepage</h2>
           My name is <a onto="[name=body]"> Richard Benjamins</a>.
</body>     </html>
```

Fig. 3.2 An early example of a schema and annotation language

accessed via the Internet. This combination of hypertext with the Internet was his actual innovation (see Fig. 3.1).

Soon this information space has grown dramatically and overgrown all competing approaches. Research on the Semantic Web started in 1996 for two reasons. First, the aim has been to support the web in its nearly infinite scale. The more information added, the more machine support is needed to access relevant information pieces. In Fensel et al. (1997, 2000), we described a Semantic Web system based on a schema [Ontology (Studer et al. 1998)], annotations of content (based on an annotation language called HTML-A), and reasoning engines and crawlers to access and process the available information (see also Fig. 3.2). The second goal was to solve the knowledge acquisition bottleneck, bringing AI back in the game and create a brain for humanity (cf. Fensel and Musen 2001). Billions of humans put data, information, and knowledge on this global network for free. Through this, the web mirrors large fractions of human knowledge, and a new brain of humanity based on the knowledge of humankind is generated. Empowered by semantics, a computer can access and understand this knowledge. This vision of the Semantic Web has been to build *a brain of/for humankind*. CYC would finally work if large fractions of humanity were joining this task for free. It just requires annotating content with semantic information.

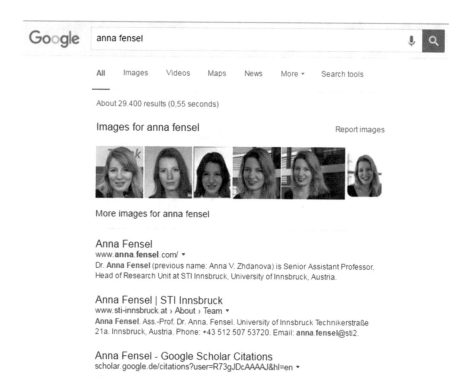

Fig. 3.3 Google as a search engine

Unfortunately, around the millennium change, web search engines arose that chose a different approach for information access on the web. They were basing their operations on syntax and statistical analysis. Some of them performed quite amazing in retrieving a proper list of links to follow given a keyword as an input. See an example of this performance in Fig. 3.3. Statistical analysis of web resources is enough to provide a fast and excellent index system for the web. Search engines such as Google did not need semantics for this and turned into an opponent of such approaches.

Initially, the business model was quite simple. Ads on the Google site brought revenue because more and more users used Google as the starting point for their web surfing. After they found an interesting link, they left the Google side and manually extracted information from the websites they visited. This *search engine* business model was hugely successful but finally limited. The users left the Google site as soon as they entered. Therefore, step by step, Google has been aiming at turning from a search engine into a *query-answering engine* (see Guha et al. 2003; Harth et al. 2007). Why point visitors to other websites? Why not provide the answer to their queries directly at the Google results keeping them there and opening new opportunities for commercial cooperation with them (see Fig. 3.4)? However, this requires more intelligence at the side of Google. It must be able to extract exact

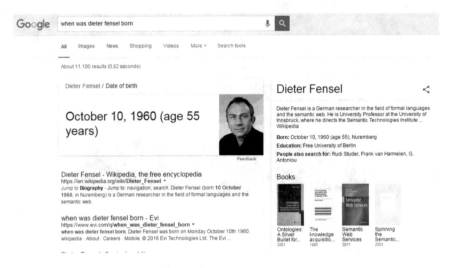

Fig. 3.4   Google as a query-answering engine

information from a website based on machine-processable semantics of content and data. Achieving this goal asks for more elaborated approaches than simple matrix manipulations.

In consequence, around 2011 a coalition of leading search engines started the *schema.org*[7] initiative that allows the injection of semantic annotations in HTML code based on JSON-LD, Microdata, and RDFa syntax. Meanwhile, a mature corpus of types, properties, range restrictions, and enumeration values have been developed, and the uptake is significant. Any important website is using it. Based on the annotations, Google develops its *Google Knowledge Graph*, a knowledge base containing already around 100 billion facts about more than 1 billion entities. What proof of figures that the knowledge acquisition bottleneck is bypassed! Meanwhile, Google went a step further and identified *Artificial Intelligence* as a critical competence needed for its future prosperity (see Fig. 3.5).

Based on this, new ways to present information from *external* sources in a structured way become possible. See, for example, the possibilities of rich snippets (Fig. 3.6), carousels, or event tables.

> Google's Knowledge Graph is perhaps most visible when users issue queries about entities, and the search results include an array of facts about the entities that are served from the Knowledge Graph. For example, a query for "I.M. Pei" produces a small panel in the search results with information about the architect's education, awards, and the significant structures he designed (Noy et al. 2019).

Such a concept offers entirely new ways of presenting information and doing e-marketing and e-commerce. It is what is occasionally called the "headless web."[8]

---

[7]https://schema.org/

[8]https://paul.kinlan.me/the-headless-web/

In der Manier des Apple-Gründers: *Googles Vorstandschef Sundar Pichai bei der Produktvorstellung in San Francisco* Foto Reuters

Fig. 3.5 Google reference to AI

Information is presented without a URL as reference. Content gets extracted from other pages and directly represented without its original layout representation. Many web page design aspects become irrelevant as robots visit the pages and not humans. Necessary for being perceived is the publication of high-quality, well-structured, and semantically annotated content. This will soon become a dominant access layer on top of the more-than-25-year-old web. Spoken in a nutshell, in 5 years no kid will know the web (with the exceptions of students of history). This significantly alters a core principle of the web and opens new opportunities to channel and bundle commercial activities. Take a look at a recent search with Google shown in Fig. 3.7. Only around 25% of the result shows classical web resources. The remainder is paid advertisement and a Google-based e-commerce solution. This goes a step further with the Google Assistant on mobile devices where traditional web results are nearly no longer shown at all but only content selected and aggregated by Google.

Moreover, Google is, by far, not the only player in this game. The current hype around chatbots and Intelligent Personal Assistants targets this new access layer on top of the web. Alexa, Bixby, Cortana, Facebook messenger, Google Assistant, Siri, and others provide personalized and (spoken) message-based access to information. This generates new challenges for providers that need to make their content, data, and services visible to potential customers.

Like it was a *must* 20 years ago to communicate via email and be visible on the web, it is now crucial for economic success to be present properly in this new, dialog-based information access. We identify four major challenges for achieving such a goal.

Best ever chunky guacamole recipe | BBC Good Food

https://www.bbcgoodfood.com/recipes/9088/bestever-chunky-guacamole ▾

 ★★★★★ Rating: 4,8 - 122 votes - 10 mins - 103 cal

This is the best version of this classic dip. The ingredients are kept to a minimum, so it's as fresh-tasting as possible, from BBC Good Food.

Guacamole Recipe | Alton Brown | Food Network

https://www.foodnetwork.com › Recipes › Alton Brown ▾

 ★★★★★ Rating: 4,8 - 878 reviews - 1 hr 20 mins - 172 cal

In a large bowl place the scooped avocado pulp and lime juice, toss to coat. Drain, and reserve the lime juice, after all of the avocados have been coated. ... Then, fold in the onions, tomatoes, cilantro, and garlic.

Best Ever Guacamole (Fresh, Easy & Authentic) | Downshiftology

https://downshiftology.com/recipes/best-ever-guacamole/ ▾

 ★★★★★ Rating: 5 - 61 votes - 10 mins - 184.8 cal

Apr 19, 2019 - This is the BEST **guacamole** recipe as it's is simple to make and uses fresh, high quality ingredients. Authentic **guacamole** doesn't contain fillers ...

The BEST Guacamole Recipe! | Gimme Some Oven

https://www.gimmesomeoven.com/perfect-guacamole/ ▾

 ★★★★★ Rating: 5 - 20 reviews - 5 mins

Mar 6, 2019 - Instructions. Mash together avocados, jalapeno, onion, lime juice, cilantro, salt, cumin with a fork until well-mixed. Serve immediately, or cover the bowl with plastic wrap (so that the plastic is literally touching the entire top layer of the **guacamole**) and refrigerate for up to 2 days before serving.

HOTEL NEUHAUS SUPERIOR: Bewertungen, Fotos ... - TripAdvisor

https://www.tripadvisor.at › ... › Hotels Saalbach-Hinterglemm ▾

★★★★★ Bewertung: 4,5 - 207 Rezensionen - Preisspanne: €€ (Basierend auf den durchschnittlichen Preisen unserer Partner pro Nacht für ein Standardzimmer)

Hotel Neuhaus Superior, Saalbach-Hinterglemm: 207 Bewertungen, 167 authentische Reisefotos und günstige Angebote für **Hotel Neuhaus** Superior.

Hotel Alpendomizil Neuhaus (Mayrhofen) • HolidayCheck (Tirol ...

https://www.holidaycheck.at › Europa › Österreich › Tirol › Mayrhofen ▾

★★★★★ Bewertung: 4,9/6 - 272 Abstimmungsergebnisse

Bewertungen, Hotelbilder & TOP Angebote: **Hotel** Alpendomizil **Neuhaus** √100€ Gutschein √Bestpreis-Garantie √GRATIS ☎ Hotline √Preisvergleich ✈ Urlaub ...

Das Neuhaus (Saalbach-Hinterglemm) • HolidayCheck (Salzburger ...

https://www.holidaycheck.at › ... › Salzburger Land › Saalbach-Hinterglemm ▾

★★★★★ Bewertung: 5,7/6 - 226 Abstimmungsergebnisse

Das **Hotel** allgemein. Erleben Sie einen Mix aus zeitloser Klassik und Design. Mit viel Liebe zum Detail bieten wir Ihnen ein Urlaubszuhause mit einem ...

Fig. 3.6 Examples of rich snippets for recipes and hotels

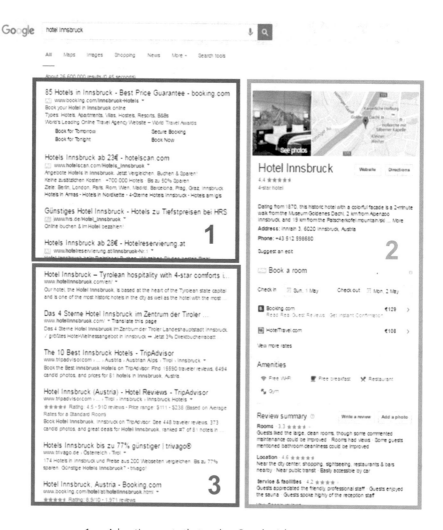

1. Advertisements that makes Google rich.
2. Direct eCommerce that will make Google even richer (Google hotel ads, limited offers, places, maps, etc.).
3. Google 1.0, the historical Web.

Fig. 3.7 Search for "Hotel Innsbruck" with Google

- You need to understand user requests precisely. Beyond simple stimulus-response patterns communication based on simple query answering, you should be able to organize a goal-oriented dialog with them.
- You need to have access to vast sources of smart content, data, and services. Their smartness is based on adequately structured and semantically (i.e., machine

processable) metadata. Only this enables knowledgeable dialogs with your potential customers. No knowledge, no power, as we know from history.

- Proper matchmaking of intents identified by Natural Language Processing technologies with semantically annotated resources is needed. Here, two types of semantic technologies (understanding human language and making resources machine-understandable) shake hands.
- Steady improvement and adaptation of achieved solutions through semi-automatic and fully automatic techniques. Something that is called machine learning.

All challenges are primarily based on the progress in Artificial Intelligence, which suddenly turned from a pariah discipline into something everybody wants and must have. It is a bit like with windmills. First, Don Quixote was fighting against them without success. Then they became a piece for museums of technological history, and finally, they are state-of-the-art technology to generate electricity. In many aspects, science has periodic changes of taste, like the fashion industry has, too.

3.2.3 Summary

In Berners-Lee et al. (2001), the authors envisaged a web where no longer humans but bots are accessing information on the web, and these bots are supporting humans in fulfilling their tasks. Content, data, and services must be enriched with machine processable semantics to be accessible by these bots. Additionally, bots must understand humans. Natural language processing must be improved toward a level where smooth automated interaction can be provided. We want to improve current techniques to identify intents in human communication acts and develop methods for structured and goal-oriented communications using information about the context of the user as well as machine-processable semantics of the available resources. This defines several research questions which will be discussed further during the following sections.

3.3 Knowledge Access Layer

For example, current knowledge graphs fall short on representing time, versioning, probability, fuzziness, context, reification, and handling inconsistency among others. New generations of knowledge graph models should explain/describe/implement these and other aspects of the structure of "knowledge & data at scale". (Groth et al. 2019)

Knowledge management technology based on graph-based repositories (see Chap. 2) is responsible for acquiring, storing, and managing Knowledge Graphs together with context data on user requests. We implement the connection of user request with resources through *inference engines* based on deductive reasoning (see

Ramakrishnan and Ullman 1995). They implement agents that define views on this graph together with data from user requests and external data sources. The inference engines access this information to obtain data for their reasoning that provides input to the dialog engine interacting with the human user.

In this section, we first introduce this as a new concept for TBoxes that are not one monolithic layer on top of very large ABoxes but as specialized means to work with a defined subset of the Knowledge Graphs for fulfilling certain tasks in specific domains. Second, we focus on the handling of dynamic and active data. Dynamic data cannot simply be stored in the Knowledge Graph as they steadily change over time. We need to access them during query-answering time through semantic descriptions of external information sources. With active data, we refer to the fact that a reservation or booking action does also change the state of an external source.

3.3.1   Loosely Connected TBoxes Defining Logic-Based Views on Knowledge Graphs

Reasoning is about discovering new knowledge from existing one. It starts with one or more general premises and links them to reach specific conclusions. It operates on logical propositions that may be either true or false (Sternberg and Sternberg 2009). If the premises are true, then we conclude that the conclusions are true, too. It is not an easy task, especially when confronted with ambiguous, contradictory, misclassified, and uncertain knowledge (Reed and Pease 2017). While ambiguity can be clarified by using context to infer the intended meaning, discovering contradictions requires theorem-proving techniques that become challenging when the knowledge base increases in size. Identification and reclassification of misclassified knowledge are also needed, as well as the incorporation of probabilities into reasoning to deal with uncertainty. Automatic reasoning started with theorem proving of variants of first-order logic in the early days of Artificial Intelligence (compare Kowalski 1974). The restriction to horn logic allowed simplified calculi and led to the logic programming language Prolog.[9] Alternatively, production rule systems[10] have been developed that also provided a rule-based syntax, however, without any declarative semantics. The complexity of reasoning in these systems, as well as the wish to define model theoretical semantics, led to the development of description logics (Baader et al. 2017) and deductive databases (Kifer et al. 1995). In a nutshell, description logics are binary predicate logics with restrictions on how to construct formulas. Similarly, deductive databases restrict predicate logic to Horn logic, however, they do not adopt the standard model-theoretical semantics of predicate logic. Description logics are using standard semantics of first-order logic, whereas deductive databases use variations of the minimal model semantics that allows the

---

[9]https://en.wikipedia.org/wiki/Prolog

[10]https://en.wikipedia.org/wiki/Production_system_(computer_science).

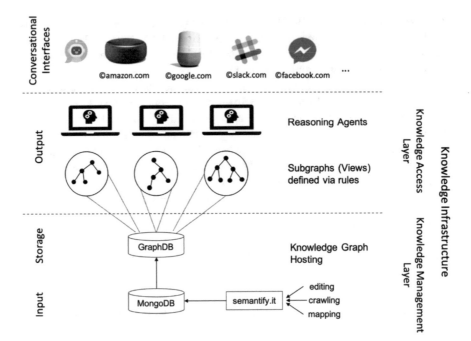

Fig. 3.8 Reasoning agents accessing a Knowledge Graph

definition of the transitive closure of a relationship. Besides Artificial Intelligence, such reasoning techniques are applied in software verification as a formal means to verify the correctness of complex software systems (see D'Silva et al. 2008). The first approach to scale reasoning practically to a scenario of *frillions* of potentially inconsistent facts that may be changing faster than any reasoning process was developed in the LarKC project; see Fensel and van Harmelen (2007) and Fensel et al. (2008).

Reasoning can be used to find errors, correct errors, and enrich the knowledge in a Knowledge Graph (Paulheim 2017). However, here, we focus on the aspect of creating personalized, dialog-oriented access to large Knowledge Graphs. A graph database is used to store the Knowledge Graph. On top of the repository, so-called reasoning agents use parts of the Knowledge Graph to handle user requests. Figure 3.8 presents a schematic representation of the architecture, including the Knowledge Graph and the reasoning agents. For example, the Knowledge Graph contains all the knowledge about ski resorts in Austria. In order to build a chatbot for Wilder Kaiser, only the data from Wilder Kaiser are needed. Therefore, a new reasoning agent will be created, which uses only the data from Wilder Kaiser.

Rules can play different roles in dialog-based systems using Knowledge Graphs. First, rules allow for expressing complex bearings in an Ontology. For instance, which ski areas are connected via ski slopes and the total length of all ski slopes in an area can be expressed by rules. Reasoning dynamically deduces the answers using those rules. Second, dialog modeling is a complex undertaking in complex domains and for complex processes. Reasoning uses the context, the previous answers, and the Knowledge Graph to create flexible and intelligent dialogs. Third, reasoning allows integrating external knowledge sources and services context into the answers. As we work with huge sets of facts, requirements are high performance and scalable real-time reasoning. Means for that in databases are properly partitioning the data, parallel, federated, clustered, and distributed query answering.[11] The advantage of using parts of the data in the reasoning agents is that these agents can optimize the reasoning process to improve the performance and can decrease the response times. Defining such views that constitute a *knowledge access layer*[12] has many advantages:

---

[11]A method to reduce the response time is, for example, so-called magic sets (Bancilhon et al. 1986). The idea behind magic sets is that the existing rules will be adapted so that they do not create facts which are useless for the response. The magic sets will persist as long as the data stays the same. So the Knowledge Graph can be updated permanently, whereas the agent takes periodical snapshots that are then compiled in an optimized presentation. However, dynamic data such as streams must be directly incorporated and require stream-reasoning approaches (see Dell'Aglio et al. 2017).

[12]"We can start with Newtonian mechanics. For a couple of centuries, scientists and philosophers thought that Newton's laws ($F = ma$ and related equations) were the ultimate Theory of Everything (ToE). They thought that those laws were the fundamental axioms, and every term $T(x, y, z...)$ in science could be defined by statement of the following form: $T(x, y, z...)$ if and only if some expression $P(x, y, z...)$, where P is some combination of statements in Newtonian mechanics that involve the variables $x, y, z...$

The first cracks in that claim came in the nineteenth century with Maxwell's equations for electromagnetism, which were independent of $F = ma$. That led to major research efforts, which led to various equations that the physicists and mathematicians were trying to integrate with $F = ma$. But their attempts created all sorts of loose ends.

In 1905, Einstein published some critical papers that used those equations. He kept $F = ma$ as a fundamental assumption, and he related the equations for the other loose ends. But the results (relativity and quantum mechanics) caused all the definitions of F, m, a, and their relationships to change. For over a century, scientists have been using the same words: force, mass, position, velocity, acceleration, momentum, energy... But *every* definition of those words has changed with every new discovery and explanation (theory). Furthermore, the most fundamental definition of mass involves the recently discovered Higgs boson. That's the closest thing to a ToE. But nobody would ever dream of using that definition for any practical application of any kind. In fact, Newton's equations, which are at best approximately true, are still the most widely used for most purposes. But any large system will include many components that use multiple inconsistent approximations.

Your car, for example, was designed with Newton's equations for all major motions, including the engine, steering, brakes, and springs. But all the electrical and electronic equipment depends on Maxwell's equations, which are fundamentally relativistic. The fire in a gasoline engine or the chemical reactions in the battery depend on quantum-mechanical calculations. Any GPS signals it may use depend on relativistic corrections for the signals from satellites. And all those computations are so complex, that they use special-case approximations that are inconsistent with the special cases assumed for the others.

Basic principle: Your car, cell phone, refrigerator, TV... are based on a multiplicity of inconsistent theories with inconsistent definitions. There is no single unified ontology that could be used to specify every feature of any of them. Even if somebody might discover a universal ToE, the calculations that depend on it would be at least as complex as anything that depends on the Higgs boson. Don't expect anything better during the twenty-first century, if ever.

- Instead of accessing trillions of facts, an access layer can provide a much more reduced amount of them.
- It is not necessary to curate the entire Knowledge Graphs in terms of aspects like inconsistencies. It can be used as a semantic data lake[13] allowing different views on data. Each reasoning agent can restrict itself to a well-curated island.
- Access rights and privacy issues may prevent specific applications to access the entire Knowledge Graph but only subsets of it. This can be implemented by these views.
- It integrates additional dynamic knowledge sources and user-given input.

This extends the architecture that was discussed in Sect. 2.4, distinguishing three layers of different functionalities (see Fig. 3.8).[14]

- *Input*: We use at the input layer MongoDB extended by crawlers and semantify it. APIs collect and semantically lift data from various sources.
- *Storage*: These data are stored as facts in the Knowledge Graph, curated, and hosted by GraphDB.
- *Output*: The data are accessible through personalized agents that define partial views[15] on the Knowledge Graph and providing contextual and personalized reasoning on top of these data [also called *personalized fusion* in Dong and Naumann (2009)].
- Finally, a *conversational interface* on top of the knowledge infrastructure manages the dialog-specific aspects of an application.

Interestingly, our Knowledge Access Layer could be viewed as a reintroduction of the *TBox*; however, in a distributed and localized version. Instead of trying to find axioms and rules that hold for the entire world, it extends a subset of the Knowledge Graph in a defined context. All the problems around defining such global logical expressions for the entire world with all their heterogeneity, inconsistency, and notorious exceptions are bypassed by reducing the scope of such rules that should govern the *ABox*. These also make them comparable to so-called inference actions in the CommonKADS methodology (Schreiber et al. 2000) and microtheories in CYC (Guha 1991).[16]

If anybody wants a truly universal explanation of everything, you can rely on the all-time favorite: God. As the mathematician Paul Erdős said, he hoped that when he died he would have a chance to look into God's Big Book. It would be nice if he did." J. F. Sowa, email at ontology-summit@googlegroups.com, Sat, 1 Jun 2019 15:46:21–0400.

[13]https://en.wikipedia.org/wiki/Data_lake

[14]A more direct coupling is proposed in Marx et al. (2014).

[15]Using a local-as-view approach, for example, used in Infomaster (Genesereth et al. 1997). For a general discussion, see also Bleiholder and Naumann (2009).

[16]See also Brachman (1990).

3.3.2 Dynamic and Active Data: Semantic Web Services

Knowledge Graphs and applications working with them deal with three different types of data:

- *Static data* are data that do not likely change frequently. For instance, the address of a hotel or the birthdate of a person do not change very often. This low velocity allows to directly store these data in a Knowledge Graph repository.
- *Dynamic data* change with a high frequency, for instance, age, weather forecast, traffic information, or share prices. Here the actual data must be accessed periodically or on demand. It is possible to store these data for future data mining, but the current data must be accessed dynamically.
- *Active data*, which changing the state of an *external* resource. For instance, a booking action changes the state of an external resource (e.g., creation of new room reservations at a hotel).

For both dynamic and active data, web services play an important role. For dynamic data like temperature at a given location and time, a request (e.g., HTTP GET) to the weather web service must be made to retrieve the necessary information at the query time. Similarly, for active data, a request (e.g., HTTP PUT) to a hotel's booking web service must be sent to make a room reservation.

Traditionally, applications would hardwire the logic to consume web services into their business logic. In order to utilize services automatically, the web service descriptions should be semantically enriched (Ankolekar et al. 2002; Fensel and Bussler 2002) and stored in the Knowledge Graphs. Unlike static data, a Knowledge Graph stores the *semantic annotations* of the service with which it needs to interact and not the data directly. Intelligent applications like conversational interfaces then access the web services on the fly. In this section, we give an overview of the Semantic Web services technology that enables semantic description of web services and consequently automated consumption by applications, allowing them to integrate dynamic and active data.

We first introduce the so-called heavyweight approaches, targeting mainly SOAP web services, and then we dive into the so-called lightweight approaches that enable semantic descriptions of RESTful web services.

The Internet Reasoning Service (IRS-II) (Motta et al. 2003) provides an infrastructure for publication, storage, composition, and execution of heterogeneous web services with the help of semantic descriptions. IRS-II matches implementation independent descriptions of different reasoning process to relevant tasks. IRS-II stands out with its advanced publication and registry mechanisms.

OWL-S uses OWL and description logic (DL) for describing web services (Martin et al. 2004). It utilizes three main elements: the service profile to describe the capabilities provided by a web service and some nonfunctional aspects, process model to describe order of service calls need to be made to perform a certain task, and service grounding to enable the description of concrete WSDL bindings for invocation.

METEOR-S (Patil et al. 2004) framework supports the whole Semantic Web services lifecycle by describing data, functional, nonfunctional, and execution semantics. The METEOR-S framework extends existing web and web services technologies for semantic descriptions. It adopts the SAWSDL (Semantic Annotations of Web Services) (Kopecký et al. 2007) technology for annotating WSDL services. METEOR-S provides tools for design, discovery, composition, and execution of web services.

Developed based on the insights obtained from the OWL-S, the Semantic Web Services Framework (SWSF) (Battle et al. 2005) provides a more expressive framework by using first-order logic (FOL) instead of DL, sacrificing decidability. The framework uses the Semantic Web Services Ontology (SWSO) for the conceptual modeling and the Semantic Web Services Language to express SWSO. Moreover, SWSF extends the Process Specification Language (PSL)[17] for defining process flow of web services.

The Web Service Modelling Framework (WSMF) (Fensel and Bussler 2002) provides a decoupled way of automating the entire lifecycle of web service consumption. It utilizes a conceptual model WSMO, a set of languages WSML, and an execution environment WSMX (Roman et al. 2006). WSMF has four pillars for describing web services. The first pillar, Ontologies enable domain descriptions. Goals are the second pillar which foster the description of what a user wants to do. The third pillar is the web service descriptions for describing various aspects of web services such as their capabilities and behavioral properties, and the fourth pillar mediators tackle interoperability problems at different levels.

As the RESTful web services increasingly gained popularity, the interest in Semantic Web services technology shifted toward more lightweight approaches that target such web services. An extensive survey of such approaches can be found in (Verborgh et al. 2014).

WSMO-Lite (Roman et al. 2015) is a conceptual model for describing the functionality of RESTful services in a lightweight, bottom-up manner. Unlike the approaches for SOAP services (e.g., OWL-S, WSMO), it does not follow a top-down approach but works through annotation of web service documentations (i.e., HTML file) with MicroWSMO microformat. The lightweight approach has limitations in terms of expressiveness and description of the behavioral aspects of web services. It provides a minimal model for web service descriptions to enable interoperability.

RESTDesc (Verborgh et al. 2013) focuses on the functional aspects of RESTful Web Services. It uses N3Logic (Berners-Lee and Connolly 2008) as formalism. The functionality supported on a resource can be described with pre- and post-conditions. It utilizes OPTIONS calls to resources to return the potential actions that can be taken on that resource with their expected outcomes.

Recently, two approaches, with different motivations, namely, Hydra (Lanthaler and Guetl 2013), for facilitating the creation of hypermedia-driven APIs by using

---

[17]https://en.wikipedia.org/wiki/Process_Specification_Language

linked data principles, and SmartAPI (Zaveri et al. 2017) to make APIs follow the
FAIR principles.[18] Hydra builds itself on the principle of self-documenting APIs,
meaning that a machine-readable documentation and hypermedia types are all that is
needed for a client to consume an API. SmartAPI[19] enriches some of the functional
aspects of OpenAPI[20] descriptions with semantic annotations in order to make APIs
better findable, accessible, interoperable, and reusable. Alternatively, with schema.
org Actions[21] Web API annotation may now become mainstream and integrated into
industrial de facto standards. Although it provides a generic way to describe actions
that can be taken on entities, an extended subset of actions vocabulary can be used to
describe Web APIs, and these descriptions then can natively interact with schema.
org annotations (Table 3.1). Usage of schema.org Actions is also an interesting use
case for domain specification patterns, as they provide a more task-specific (i.e., web
service description) pattern based on an otherwise generic vocabulary. Further
example Web API annotations and the domain-specific patterns can be found
online.[22] These domain-specific patterns are then used for generating an annotation
tool, including a lifting-grounding mapping for existing non-semantic APIs.[23]

3.4   Open and Service-Oriented Dialog Systems

Almost 30 years after the invention of the web, the concept of browsing as a primary
means for information access is losing its importance. With the advances of Artificial
Intelligence, content, data, and services on the web can be consumed through
conversations. If the invention of the web browser was a milestone in the history
of the web, another milestone is undoubtedly the mobile computing and conversational interfaces, especially dialog systems that work as Intelligent Personal Assistants. We first focus on the general case of Knowledge Graph-supported dialog
systems and then focus on the role of semantic description of services for building
dialog-based systems (c.f. Chen et al. 2017).

3.4.1   Open Dialog Systems

The research on dialog systems has been tackling the challenge of natural human-
computer interaction for more than 50 years (McTear et al. 2016). Although the

---

[18]https://www.go-fair.org/fair-principles/

[19]https://smart-api.info

[20]https://www.openapis.org/

[21]https://schema.org/Action/

[22]https://github.com/semantifyit/sdo-webapi

[23]https://actions.semantify.it/annotation/webApi

Table 3.1 An example action annotation for feratel API

```
{
  "@context": "http://schema.org/",
  "@type": "SearchAction",
  "actionStatus": {
    "@id": "PotentialActionStatus",
    "@type": "ActionStatusType"
  },
  "name": "Search for hotel room offers",
  "object": {
    "@type": "LodgingReservation",
    "checkinTime-input": "required",
    "checkoutTime-input": "required",
    "numAdults-input": "required"
  },
  "result": {
    "@type": [
      "HotelRoom",
      "Product"
    ],
    "name-output": "required",
    "offers": {
      "@type": "Offer",
      "name-output": "required",
      "offeredBy": {
        "type": "Hotel",
        "name-output":"required",
        "address": {
            "addressLocality-input": "required"
          }
      },
      "price-output": "required",
      "priceCurrency-output": "required"
    }
  },
  "target": {
    "@type": "EntryPoint",
    "contentType": "application/ld+json",
    "encodingType": "application/ld+json",
    "httpMethod": "POST",
    "urlTemplate":"https://actions.semantify.it/api/feratel/search"
  }
}
```

The action describes how to search hotel room offers

general architecture of a dialog system has not changed much over the years, the methods and implementation of the components in this architecture improved. Early dialog systems encoded the domain knowledge into the system, which made them relatively "closed," meaning that the adaption of such systems to new domains was very expensive. Such closeness also caused the structure of dialog being statically defined, hindering the flexible elaboration of a topic by the dialog system to collect all the necessary information to reach its goal. Knowledge bases have been used to overcome these obstacles by separating the domain knowledge from the system, allowing dialog systems to be adapted to different domains relatively more straight-forwardly (Milward and Beveridge 2003).[24] Here we want to explore the possibilities of how a Knowledge Graph based on different sources can improve a dialog system in different aspects. Like Sir Tim opened hypertext systems to the Internet, dialog systems must take the same challenge as a new access layer to information over the Internet. Google's Knowledge Graph is, in fact, one of the largest scale examples of a Knowledge Graph that powers conversational interfaces. It started by helping Google to turn into a question-answering engine, rather than a search engine (Fig. 3.9). Now it powers many Google services, including their intelligent assistant, Google Assistant.[25] From the dialog strategy perspective, dialog systems can be classified into three categories:

- System initiative systems where only the system guides the dialog
- User initiative where only the user asks the questions
- Mixed initiative where both parties can guide the dialog

Although semantic technologies have been utilized in all three categories, the main research effort in the context of the web comes for the user initiative dialog systems. Most typical user initiative dialog systems in the context of Knowledge Graphs are question-answering systems (QAS). Such systems aim to use natural language questions to retrieve information from Knowledge Graphs. According to the survey in (Diefenbach et al. 2018a), there are over 60 QAS that are powered by Knowledge Graphs on the web. In principle, these systems follow the following pipeline (Moschitti et al. 2017; Diefenbach et al. 2018a)[26]:

- Running typical NLP tasks for syntactic analysis of the question
- Entity mapping and disambiguation over the Knowledge Graph
- Query construction (e.g., SPARQL), query execution, and answer provision

Applying such a pipeline bares certain challenges at each step. A comprehensive survey (Höffner et al. 2017) on 72 publications about 62 systems on question

---

[24]For example, there is a plethora of work to improve different aspects of dialog systems, especially with machine learning in the recent years (McTear et al. 2016; Chen et al. 2017).

[25]In 2016, Google Assistant was working with Google Knowledge Graph, which contained 70 billion facts at the time (https://www.businessinsider.de/why-google-assistant-will-win-the-ai-race-2016-10?r=US&IR=T).

[26]There are also approaches such as WDAqua (Diefenbach et al. 2018b) that skip the syntactic processing step and disambiguate entities by eliminating candidate queries.

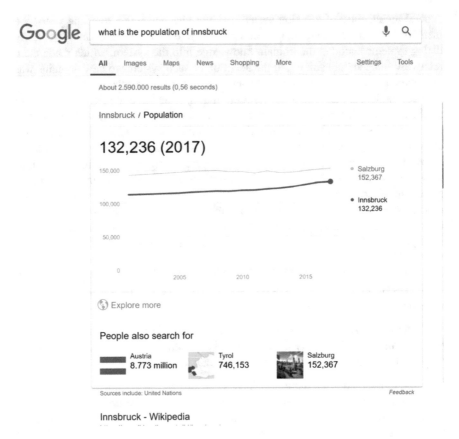

Fig. 3.9 Google as a question-answering engine

answering over the Semantic Web identifies those challenges. Following the survey, we group the most relevant ones under the following categories:

1. Lexical Gap
2. Ambiguity
3. Multilingualism
4. Complex questions and queries

In the context of question-answering systems over Knowledge Graphs, the *lexical gap* is a term for the situation where the vocabulary used in the question does not directly match the vocabulary used in the labels of the resources in a Knowledge Graph (Hakimov et al. 2015). According to the aforementioned survey, methods like string normalization and applying similarity functions, query expansion with synonyms and semantic features like hypernym-hyponym hierarchies, pattern generation for identifying various representations of relationship between two instances (i.e., different ways to represent a particular property), and incorporating traditional document retrieval methods (e.g., TF-IDF) to find relevant resources are adopted.

Ambiguity is one of the major challenges to tackle in question-answering systems. It refers to the notion of the same phrase having different meanings. As pointed out in the survey, lexical gap and ambiguity are two different sides of the same coin, since while the former affects the recall of a system, the latter has an impact on the precision. The resolution of ambiguous phrases, also known as disambiguation, aims to find the most relevant resource among multiple candidates in a Knowledge Graph to answer a natural language question. The disambiguation methods in QAS benefit from the statistical distribution of phrases in several text corpora to identify the correct context of a question. Similarly, they may benefit from the graph structure of Knowledge Graphs in order to rank the relatedness of entities. While several approaches used historical question-answer data or user context and preferences, some moved the effort mostly to the user and let them do the disambiguation of candidate answers.

Multilingualism refers to the notion of being able to handle questions and answers in multiple languages. Open Knowledge Graphs such as DBpedia and Wikidata have mappings of the data in different languages. Such mappings make a precious resource for developing multilingual QAS. Additionally, some QAS use multilingual lexicon Ontologies for answering multilingual questions.

In simple cases, QAS convert a natural language question into simple triple patterns in ASK or SELECT queries. However, *complex questions* may require queries with a more sophisticated structure (e.g., subqueries, union patterns, aggregation). The systems that can handle such complex questions benefit from pre-built linguistic representations of concepts and relations in Ontologies, determining the core elements and building queries around it, even from multiple sentences. For complex questions, template-based approaches are the most adopted ones. The generation of query templates can be manual or automated to some extent. Additional to the questions, complexity may also be introduced due to the nature of Knowledge Graphs. This typically refers to the procedural (e.g., instructions for building furniture), temporal (e.g., temporally ordered events, time-dependent facts), and spatial (e.g., spatial relationships between entities and their three-dimensional coordinates). Concepts and relationships for such aspects are usually not provided by the underlying schemas of Knowledge Graphs or not straightforward to represent with the triple-based data structure of RDF.[27] Still, some approaches try to help QAS to handle such questions by inferring such temporal and spatial relationships based on the existing knowledge.

The challenges above and different approaches tackling them pose strong evidence for the heterogeneity in addressing the question-answering challenge. As pointed out in the survey (Höffner et al. 2017), many dialog systems focus on a particular aspect of question answering. This leads to a situation where each system re-implements a certain part of the pipeline, even though there may be some components already implemented and could be reused. Researchers have addressed

---

[27]However this situation is changing. For instance, schema.org is now testing properties for spatial relationships and the Wikidata data model allows attaching temporal context to facts.

this modularity and reusability issue by providing QAS architecture and methodologies that allow building question-answering pipelines with interoperable, replaceable components in Marx et al. (2014), Singh et al. (2018), Ferrández et al. (2011) and Kim et al. (2017). An exciting approach is presented in (Singh et al. 2018), the Frankenstein framework, that integrates 29 components for different purposes in order to build question-answering pipelines. The framework integrates these components with the Qanary methodology that enables different components to share the state of the question-answering process, allowing them to interoperate. The Frankenstein framework supports dynamic pipelines, meaning the components for different tasks can be dynamically selected based on their performance according to the question type.[28]

In the remainder of this section, we have a closer look at how Knowledge Graphs can be used to improve dialog systems, in particular, Chatbots and Intelligent Personal Assistants. There are two main directions in which one can use a Knowledge Graphs for this purpose: (1) to power the language understanding part of the dialog system and (2) to react on the conversations and provide additional interactions, information, and recommendations to the user engaged in conversations with the dialog system.

When it comes to supporting the *language understanding* part of the dialog system, the goal is to use the Knowledge Graphs to provide training data for the natural language understanding service (e.g., DialogFlow[29]). We can automatically ingest from the Knowledge Graph as training data for the entity recognition task (e.g., Vienna is a city) and provide (semi-)automatically generate intents and example questions. Based on the Knowledge Graph structure, we can generate on the one hand entities and synonyms and on the other hand, intents needed in the natural language understanding service based on the entities, respectively the relations between these entities in the Knowledge Graph. Furthermore, one can use an ontology-to-text approaches to generate example questions that can be used to train the natural language understanding service.

The second direction on how Knowledge Graphs can be used to improve dialog systems is to react to the conversations and provide additional interactions, information, and recommendations to the user.

- Using the knowledge from the Knowledge Graph, the dialog system can elaborate on the topic of discussion and provide additional interesting facts. Let us consider a dialog system providing information about events. Based on the knowledge from a touristic Knowledge Graph, such a dialog system can provide the user with detailed information about an event but also additional information about the connected entities, e.g., artist, location, and means of transportation related to that event.

---

[28]Comparable to the LarKC approach that developed a similar open plug-in pipeline architecture for large-scale reasoning (Fensel et al. 2008).

[29]https://dialogflow.com/

- A Knowledge Graph can also be used to improve the handling of the conversation context. Using a template or rule-based approach, one can drive interaction with the user to provide context-dependent answers (e.g., prices based on the role of the user), the invocation of actions (booking of a hotel room with follow-up questions), or a combination of both (e.g., which outdoor events happen on the weekend if the weather permits).
- Finally, a Knowledge Graph can also be used to refine the search for products or services in a dialog system. In case the dialog system cannot answer the given question, the Knowledge Graph can be used to inquire on more information. For example, actions and APIs that are modeled as part of the Knowledge Graph might require input data of a specific type, and can be used to steer the dialog. More details on how this can be achieved are provided in the following section on service-guided dialogs/actions.

3.4.2   Service-Guided Dialogs

For goal-oriented dialog systems that aim beyond simple question answering, the external access component is usually more complicated. A goal-oriented dialog system aims to guide users to elicit all the necessary information that is needed to achieve their goal. For a dialog system that works with the data and services on the web, external communication typically involves web services. Traditionally, dialog systems are tightly coupled with the web services they access. This situation naturally brings certain limitations, for instance, service invocations are weaved into the dialog systems, and the order of the invocations are hard coded. This harms the flexibility of the dialog system, by forcing dialogs to be manually altered whenever a new service, consequently a new functionality, is introduced. This flexibility issue has implications in terms of scalability of the dialog systems that run with data and services on the web. If we see the dialog system as a client, this issue turns into a service-client decoupling challenge.

In order to utilize services automatically, the web service descriptions should be semantically enriched (Ankolekar et al. 2002; Fensel and Bussler 2002). The initial efforts were mostly focused on SOAP services [e.g., OWL-S (Martin et al. 2004); SWSF (Battle et al. 2005); WSMF (Fensel and Bussler 2002)]. Lightweight approaches targeting RESTful Web APIs have been developed in recent years to provide simple annotations for these services on the web (see Sect. 3.3.2).

We argue that a dialog system can benefit from the strengths of semantic annotation from two different viewpoints:

- First, a dialog system can generate a backend-driven intent and training sentences semi-automatically.
- Second, it can benefit from the hypermedia links of a Web API to extract the invocation flow that guides the dialog.

Table 3.2   An excerpt from an example booking conversation based on the action in Table 3.1

User:	I want a hotel room in Seefeld from 12.09.2019 to 14.09.2019
Bot:	How many guests?
User:	2
Bot:	Ok I have found following hotel rooms: 1. Double room, shower or bathtub, WC offered by Alpenpark resort for 200 EUR per night. 2. Double room, shower or bath, toilet offered by central Seefeld for 119 EUR per night. You can purchase an offer.
User:	Ok I want number 2.
. . .	. . .
Bot:	Done. Here is the reservation: . . . .

An implementation of this idea can be found in (Şimşek and Fensel 2018a). Table 3.2 shows an excerpt from an example dialog created based on an intent generated from the action annotation in Table 3.1. First the action is processed and a search intent for lodging reservation including its required parameters is created. Then user's request that already contains some of the required information for booking a room is matched with this intent. After the missing input is elicited (i.e., occupancy), the search is done via the endpoint defined in the action. The action returns hotel rooms with offers and potential buy actions attached to them. After user selects an offer, the buy action on that offer is completed and reservation is shown to the user.

The idea of extracting tasks for dialog systems from Semantic Web service descriptions is mentioned in (González Bermúdez 2010). Another system that aims to provide dialogical access to Semantic Web services is SmartWeb (Sonntag et al. 2007), a dialog-based multimodal question-answering system. The dialog system uses Semantic Web services described with OWL-S to find relevant web services to invoke according to user's request. However, the project deals with only a small set of predefined and well-curated web services. Therefore, their invocation can be hardcoded.

We utilize the schema.org vocabulary, especially the "actions" subset for describing Web APIs semantically (Şimşek et al. 2018b) (see Sect. 3.3.2). These APIs can be consumed by a dialog system semi-automatically, after their functional (e.g., operation signatures), nonfunctional (e.g., invocation fee, publisher), and behavioral (e.g., hypermedia links between resources) are mapped to schema.org.

3.4.3   Summary

Communicating with computers through natural language has been an interest of AI researchers for more than half a century. Semantic technologies have contributed to tackling various challenges of dialog system development, from natural language understanding to dialog management and external communication. Additional to the question answering over linked (open) data, Knowledge Graphs can be used to improve mixed-initiative dialog systems, especially in goal-oriented settings. This can be in terms of providing additional information regarding the topic of interest via the links between entities in a Knowledge Graph, by providing context-aware responses, or through dialogs that are driven by the semantically annotated services.

Chapter 4
Why We Need Knowledge Graphs: Applications

Abstract No matter how well curated and high quality Knowledge Graphs we build are, they are only as powerful as their applications. In this section we introduce concrete real-world use cases where Knowledge Graphs power dialog-based access to information and services. We do that by giving an overview of the existing chatbot and voice assistant market first and then demonstrating their limitations. We explain in which ways Knowledge Graphs can improve conversational interfaces with the help of pilots from different domains such as tourism and energy.

4.1 Introduction

In the previous sections, we have introduced the scientific and theoretical foundations of Knowledge Graphs, the lifecycle of Knowledge Graphs including a process model, and all tasks needed to build and maintain Knowledge Graphs as well as a Knowledge Access and Dialog-based Interface Layer to make usage out of it. This section introduces some use cases and pilots for Knowledge Graphs as a means for dialog-based access to information and services.

This section elaborates on the practical use of Knowledge Graph technologies to support applications explicitly chatbots and voice assistants and how Knowledge Graphs will unleash data for AI. The remainder of it is structured as follows. Section 4.2 provides insights into the current state of the market for chatbots and voice assistants looking at the current state/development of such solutions. Section 4.3 identifies the limitation of chatbots and voice assistants and motivates the need for a Knowledge Graph-based solution to improve dialog-based access to information. Section 4.4 exemplifies with the help of several use cases how our solution is deployed and used to power intelligent chatbots and voice assistant in tourism. Section 4.5 presents two use cases in energy domain and Sect. 4.6 expands to further verticals. Finally, we give a summary in Sect. 4.7.

© Springer Nature Switzerland AG 2020
D. Fensel et al., *Knowledge Graphs*, https://doi.org/10.1007/978-3-030-37439-6_4

4.2 The Market

The Gartner[1] hype cycle for emerging technologies (August 2018) show both Knowledge Graphs and conversational Artificial Intelligence in the innovation trigger. MarketsandMarkets[2] forecasts the global conversational AI market size to grow from USD 4.2 billion in 2019 to USD 15.7 billion by 2024, at a compound annual growth rate (CAGR) of 30% during the forecast period (2019–2024). The major growth drivers for the market include the increasing demand for AI-powered customer support services, omnichannel deployment, and reduced chatbot development cost. As we describe in the following, Knowledge Graph technologies complement Conversational Platforms to scale the automation of conversations of chatbots and voice assistant at reduced costs. The growth for conversational AI is due to the evolving usage of chatbots for content marketing activities such as digital marketing and advertising. The technological capabilities, individuality, and customization are the main features accelerating market growth. With chatbots there to assist, interact, and engage with customers, they offer personalized marketing capabilities.[3]

The 2018 State of Chatbots report shows that only 43% of consumers said they would prefer to communicate with a human. Approximately 34% said they would use a bot to connect with a human employee. Thus, the willingness to use bots is there, and a combination of the two options is conceivable.[4] Consumers would prefer a voice assistant to a website or app because it is more convenient (52%); it allows them to multitask and do things without using their hands (48%); and it helps them to make recurring purchases (41%).[5] Artificial intelligence-based voice assistance (AI-voice) will soon be a primary user interface for all digital devices—including smartphones, smart speakers, personal computers, automobiles, and home appliances. As of mid-January 2019, more than 1 billion devices worldwide were equipped with Google's AI-voice assistant,[6] and another hundred million devices spoke with Amazon's Alexa—and neither number accounts for the devices equipped with voice assistants from Apple, Microsoft, Samsung, or across the digital worlds of China and Asia. Juniper Research[7] forecasts the global market for voice assistants to

---

[1]https://gartner.com

[2]https://www.marketsandmarkets.com/Market-Reports/conversational-ai-market-49043506.html? gclid=CjwKCAjw5pPnBRBJEiwAULZKvu4Zj7wnERAAayhuZwFzcO8fquxkACCvSlAbxD8 m4tD4_BKSJAIjUhoCCmkQAvD_BwE

[3]https://www.sdcexec.com/software-technology/news/21011880/chatbot-market-to-grow-at-31-percent-cagr-from-2018-to-2024

[4]https://www.drift.com/wp-content/uploads/2018/01/2018-state-of-chatbots-report.pdf

[5]https://www.capgemini.com/consulting/wp-content/uploads/sites/30/2018/01/conversational_commerce_research_report.pdf

[6]https://voicebot.ai/2019/01/07/google-assistant-to-be-available-on-1-billion-devices-this-month-10x-more-than-alexa/

[7]https://www.juniperresearch.com/press/press-releases/digital-voice-assistants-in-use-to-triple

grow at a 25% CAGR over the next 5 years, with 8 billion active voice assistants (across all platforms and devices) by 2023. The 2019 CES Show—the world's leading exhibition of the digital future—was filled with AI-voice interfaces that ranged from the connected home to the connected car.

4.3   Motivation and Solution

Voice to text understanding has recently achieved very high accuracy and continues to improve. Nevertheless, current use cases of a chatbot and voice assistant still focus on simple question and answer solutions. A dialog with an Amazon Echo or Google Home quite often ends in "Sorry, I do not know," due to the lack of domain-specific knowledge these devices have. The reason for this is that natural language solutions of such devices lack knowledge of entities, e.g., Restaurant and Roast Pork, as demonstrated in the example in Fig. 4.1 and therefore cannot resolve the goals of the questions.

To support the chatbot and voice assistant type of scenarios introduced before, we need to design, implement, and deploy a *knowledge-centered* solution that will enable conversational interfaces to engage in human-like dialogs. Figure 4.2 depicts the internal process of such a solution for chatbots and voice assistants [also compare Singh et al. (2018)].

At first, the natural language input of a user, in written or spoken form, undergoes a natural language understanding step (understand 1), in which the user intent, together with parameters, are identified. The intent needs then to be resolved to an action that typically translates in a set of queries (map 2) that can then be executed

Fig. 4.1 Typical dialog with current chatbots and voice assistants

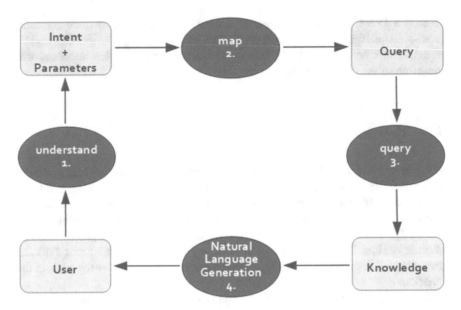

Fig. 4.2 The inner process of a knowledge-centered chatbots and voice assistants (Heuristic classification (Clancey 1985) slightly "messed" up)

(query 3) against large volumes of heterogeneous, distributed, dynamic, and potentially (i.e., nearly for sure) inconsistent statements in order to identify the relevant knowledge parts needed to generate the user answer in natural language (NLG—natural language generation 4) as text or voice; see also Höffner et al. (2017), Marx et al. (2015), and Zafar et al. (2018).

Each step of the process described above typically requires much manual work. For example, setting up the natural language understanding modules in current chatbots and voice assistants requires the intents to be designed by a human dialog manager. He/she would also need to provide example questions, also known as utterances, identify the parameters, and mark them in the utterances. The same is true for the other steps, from mapping the intents and parameters to query, to defining user's answers. In this context, the overall challenge is how to bring as much automation as possible in the process described above. The critical point is that knowledge and the usage of knowledge is the only way to address these challenges, to automatize the internal process of chatbots and voice assistants in order to deliver meaningful dialogs going beyond the current state of the art of conversational systems.

In this section, we introduce Onlim,[8] a knowledge-centered solution for conversational interfaces that follows the generic process introduced before. We show how such a knowledge-centered solution can be technically built, what the required

---

[8]https://www.onlim.com/

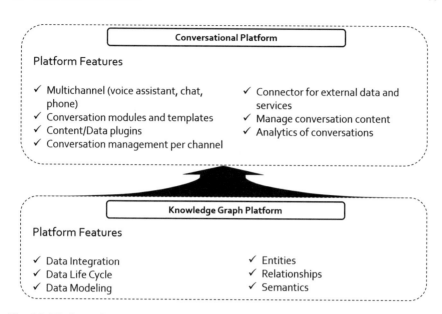

Fig. 4.3 The internal process of a knowledge-centered chatbots and voice assistants

building blocks are, and how they fit together. Figure 4.3 shows the two main building blocks, i.e., the Conversational Platform and the Knowledge Graph Platform.

The Conversational Platform is the place supporting the full lifecycle of chatbots and voice assistants, including but not limited to setup and management. This platform enables easy deployment of the conversational agent on a multitude of channels, from Facebook Messenger, chatbot widget that can be integrated on the website, to voice channels such as Alexa and Google Assistant on phone interfaces. The Conversational Platform includes conversational modules and templates needed to generate answers, as well as to manage conversations and perform analytics on conversational data. A strong feature of the Conversational Platform is the possibility to integrate external data and service, as well as to plug in content and data for conversations.

This Conversational Platform is powered by the knowledge available in the *Knowledge Graph Platform*. This second platform relies on the following blocks: *Semantics, Knowledge Graphs, Algorithms,* and *Applications.*

Semantics is at the backbone of this solution, enabling the capturing of the meaning of data as well as of the customer's domain information. Furthermore, semantics enables the smart matchmaking between customer requests in natural language and appropriate answers related to the channel. To realize the unified semantic representation of the customer's domain information, we use semantic technologies to capture industry-specific information about the customer in the form of a domain model. We use these models specific for each domain or industry sector that defines the information or knowledge items. We based our models on schema.

org. We support various schemas, define a unifying schema, and map other schemas into it. As our models are already based on schema.org, we use schema.org as unifying schema and extend it with additional types and properties to fit our needs.[9]

A *Knowledge Graph* is a self-descriptive knowledge base where data and its schema are stored in a graph format, and the relations/connections between data are first-class citizens. This data representation allows for flexible data modeling and reducing the data integration complexity (e.g., by merely creating new links between data sources). It also allows us to apply a broad set of applications and algorithms. In order to get knowledge in our Knowledge Graphs, we follow the knowledge creation methods described in Sect. 2.2, taking as input a variety of data sources. We have implemented a software solution that retrieves data from multiple content sources in various formats, e.g., XML, CSV, and JSON, via APIs, in a pull or push approach, and generates semantic annotations according to a unified semantic representation based on schema.org and extensions. Conceptual mappings are created between the various schemas and our internal schema. Previous work is done in the field of Ontology mapping, and Ontology alignment is used as a foundation for our solution (cf. Studer et al. 1998; Staab and Studer 2010). Mappings require a mapping language to specify the conceptual mappings and a mapping engine to execute the mappings between the schemas (cf. Şimşek et al. (2019a) and Sect. 2.2.3.3).

Algorithms that run on top of Knowledge Graphs include inference, recommendations, machine learning, and text understanding, to name a few. Given the semantic representation of entities and relationships between them that are represented as part of the Knowledge Graph, inference algorithms, of various complexity, e.g., rule-based reasoning, OWL/RDFS reasoning, or combinations of these approaches, can be used to infer knowledge and enrich the Knowledge Graph. This increases the knowledge by creating and inferring new relations (e.g., identifying hotels, which also have a restaurant by mapping via the location). Another class of algorithms that can be applied on top of Knowledge Graphs are recommendations algorithms. We use the structure and semantics of data to generate knowledge for chatbots and voice assistants in the form of entities and actions and combine this with personalization. Profile information extracted from various sources (e.g., Facebook profiles or CRM systems) is represented as rules and used to identify the relevant content and send it in a personalized form to a user. This leads to more relevant content, additional interesting facts, in the short term better recommendations for a user and better results for content providers, as well as, over time, smarter chatbot systems. Finally, the Knowledge Graphs structure can be used to power text understanding and machine learning algorithms. Here we use the Knowledge Graphs to provide training data for the Natural Language Understanding service (e.g., Dialogflow[10]). We can automatically derive from the Knowledge Graph training data for entity recognition (e.g., Telfs is a village) and provide (semi-)automatically generated intents and example questions. Dialogs refer to template or rule-based

---

[9]https://schema-tourism.sti2.org/

[10]https://dialogflow.com/

descriptions how the chatbot interacts with the user to provide context-dependent answers (e.g., prices based on the profile of the user), the invocation of actions (booking of a hotel with follow-up questions), or a combination of both (e.g., which outdoor events happen on the weekend if the weather permits).

Applications, more precisely chatbots and voice assistants, are fed with knowledge from the Knowledge Graph in order to better answer human users' natural language queries and engage in meaningful dialogs with them.

Let us revisit our example in Fig. 4.1 and see how Knowledge Graphs can enable chatbots and voice assistants to understand the goal the human users expressed in natural language requests. Figure 4.4 illustrates the different steps of the process, from understanding the user request to generating and executing the query against the Knowledge Graph, to generating the answer for the user. With a touristic Knowledge Graph in place that includes touristic entities such as restaurants, offers of these restaurants (e.g., roast pork), as well as actions related to these entities that can be performed (e.g., booking a table), intents and parameters can be derived. For example, an intent *TableReservation* for entities of type Restaurant can be generated. Restaurants and, in general, organizations can be connected in the Knowledge Graphs to other entities of type Offer (e.g., Roast Pork offers).

Further, the Knowledge Graph can be used to improve the understanding of the NLU by pushing entities from the Knowledge Graph (e.g., Hofbräu Bierhaus NYC) to the NLU or by generating example questions for the intents. The Knowledge Graph can also be used to generate the rules that restrict the view/access to the Knowledge Graph depending on the use cases. Such rules, together with the intent and parameters extracted by the NLU, are used to generate the queries to be executed against the Knowledge Graph. Last but not least, the Knowledge Graph can be used to generate templates for the answers, textual answers, or follow-up questions to run the dialogs.

4.4 Touristic Use Cases

Here we introduce use cases for Knowledge Graphs as a means for dialog-based access to information and services in the tourism area, namely, touristic chatbots and voice assistants that are using Knowledge Graphs to achieve a better understanding of natural language dialogs.[11] We look at different application scenarios and describe requirements that must be fulfilled with the help of Knowledge Graph technology.

Chatbots and voice assistants have started to play an increasing role in customer communication for many businesses in various verticals. Especially in tourism, they are proving more and more benefits in terms of convenience, availability, and fast

---

[11]Note that tourism is one of the most important economical verticals on a worldwide scale, accounting for around 10% of the global GDP and total employment in 2017 (WTTC 2018).

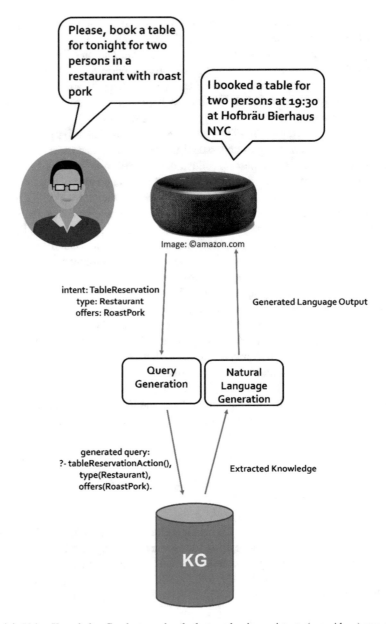

Fig. 4.4 Using Knowledge Graphs to make chatbots and voice assistants (e.g., Alexa) smarter

access to information and customer support through the entire customer journey.[12] In the *dreaming and planning phase*, hotels and Destination Management

[12]https://tourismeschool.com/customer-journey-mapping-tourism-brands/

Organizations (DMOs) can provide information through chatbots and voice assistants about the hotel and the region, the surroundings, and weather conditions to potential guests. In the *booking phase*, from booking the hotel and transport to buying connected services, e.g., ski tickets, all becomes much simpler and efficient by using natural language. Finally, in the *experiences phase*, chatbots and voice assistants can also announce special offers or events. All requested information and processes are available 24/7/365 and instantly. For hotels guests, in particular, the stay experience can be enriched by providing them access to hotel services and beyond. Recently Amazon launched a program for hotel operators[13] that allows guests to request room service, ask for housekeeping, configure the temperature and lights in the hotel room, set wake-up calls, and even connect their accounts to listen to their music and audiobooks.

Finally, customer support questions regarding rooms, equipment, additional services, and more are answered in a fully automated way. One can argue that similar functionalities are available in mobile apps, but the major drawback of these apps is that each of them is focusing on different aspects, and one needs some time to learn how each app is working. Chatbots and voice assistants provide more straightforward means to access the same functionalities by using the most natural way for humans to interact, i.e., natural language (as voice or written text).

Touristic chatbots and voice assistants are thus expected to answer questions of different nature from "What is the most popular attraction in the city?", "What events are happening the coming weekend?", "What is the snow height?" to "Book me a table tonight for 2 persons in a Tyrolean restaurant," "I am looking for a bike ride that is difficult and offers huts on the way," and so forth. To correctly answer all these types of questions and perform tasks such as booking, chatbots and voice assistants need machine-processable (semantic) annotations of content, data, and services. They need structures that encode the knowledge about the tourism domain, in terms of entities and relations between them, in a machine-processable form. Knowledge Graphs are such structure providing the technical means to integrate various heterogeneous touristic information sources, for instance, about accommodations, points of interests (POI),[14] events, and sports activity locations. With the help of Knowledge Graphs, not only simple question-answering tasks can be supported but rather complex conversations/dialogs.

Applying the principles, methods, and tools introduced in the previous sections, we have built a Knowledge Graph for Tourism that integrates multiple sources of content, data, and services from various providers:

---

[13]https://techcrunch.com/2018/06/19/amazon-launches-an-alexa-system-for-hotels/

[14]A very interesting approach for POI data integration in open, heterogeneous, and distributed data sources is described in Athanasiou et al. (2019a). The approach described here is more focusing on proprietary data sources, but certain aspects of this technological approach can also be reused in such a more simple setting.

- Closed sources: feratel,[15] General Solutions,[16] intermaps,[17] Outdooractive,[18] and Verkehrsauskunft Österreich[19]
- Open sources: DBpedia,[20] GeoNames,[21] OpenStreetMap,[22] and Wikidata[23]

The resulting touristic Knowledge Graph powers several chatbots and voice assistants of touristic regions in Tyrol, Austria. The *Seefeld pilot*[24] focuses on integrating only closed data sources, namely, from feratel, General Solutions, Intermaps, and Outdooractive. The use case is for the Olympiaregion Seefeld. For this use case, we also focus on question answering for more advanced (compound) questions. For instance, "Where can I have a traditional Tyrolean food when going cross country skiing?" (see Fig. 4.5).

The Serfaus-Fiss-Ladis tourist region envisions that users can not only chat about the specific tourism data but also inquire on common knowledge about the region. The conversational interface can handle questions that are combining the closed and open datasets. For instance, "How many inhabitants does Serfaus have?" or "Traffic information from Serfaus to Via Claudia Augusta?" (see Fig. 4.6).

Common to all these pilots and use cases is the need to integrate data from multiple heterogeneous static and dynamic sources for which we need to track provenance (e.g., data owner, temporal validity, or the integration process) and maintain one shared evolving schema. Using knowledge cleaning and enrichment, we also ensured a certain level of quality of the touristic knowledge. The ultimate aim is to optimize conversational interfaces based on Knowledge Graphs by providing a rich intent and entity management (e.g., automated NLU training), question answering over the Knowledge Graph, and supporting advanced dialogs such as guiding a user through actions or recommendations or follow-up conversations.

In detail, this requires:

1. *Integration of data from multiple sources:* Common to all use cases and pilots is that data from different sources need to be combined and integrated into one coherent data model. Also, new data sources will be added in the future. Representing the information (facts and relationships between facts) in the form of one large Knowledge Graph seems natural and provides the necessary flexibility to integrate new data sources and enrich existing information with new relationships. This also requires creating and maintaining one large data schema

---

[15]http://www.feratel.at/en/

[16]https://general-solutions.eu/

[17]https://www.intermaps.com/en/

[18]https://www.outdooractive.com/

[19]https://verkehrsauskunft.at/

[20]https://wiki.dbpedia.org/

[21]https://www.geonames.org/

[22]https://www.openstreetmap.org

[23]https://www.wikidata.org/

[24]https://www.seefeld.com/en/

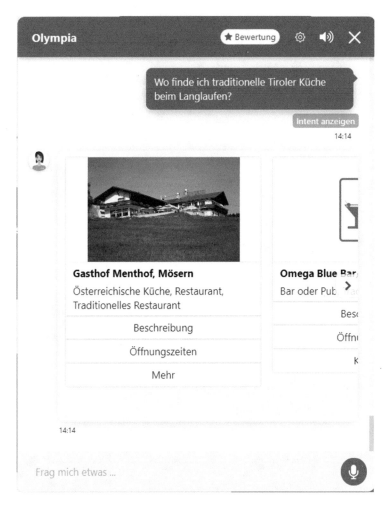

Fig. 4.5 Seefeld pilot

for existing and new sources and verify that the schema and data are consistent and that the imported data adheres to our schema.

2. *Static and dynamic information:* The data sources can provide static information (e.g., geolocations, names, categories) but also dynamic information (e.g., the current weather, snow level, open ski lifts, hotel rates, or transport information). Therefore, our solution must handle and represent such dynamic information, by combining updates in the Knowledge Graph and by specifying services to derive the current and most up-to-date information.

3. *Represent facts and available services/actions:* The Knowledge Graph needs to contain not only facts but also the description of actions and services (active data). For instance, given the hotel domain, we do not only need to represent and search over hotel information but also describe the actions related to hotels, such as

Fig. 4.6 Serfaus-Fiss-Ladis pilot

booking a hotel room or additional services offered by the hotel. The service descriptions should contain not only the service type but also all information which allows invoking such a service. This includes the description of the service protocol, required and optional parameters, and the response information.

4. *Clean and enrich existing knowledge:* The Knowledge Graph must further be cleaned and enriched. The cleaning steps typically contain the handling of duplicate information, entity resolution, or linking and checking for introduced inconsistencies (e.g., different sets of opening hours for the same hotel). The next step is to further enrich this knowledge by creating new relations between entities. First, this is done to add missing links (e.g., adding a booking service to a hotel or geolocation information to an address) and second, to connect entities with

additional and new links (e.g., adding an inWalkingDistance link between hotels and restaurants based on some predefined measures).

5. *Track provenance of data sources.* One important aspect is to track and represent provenance information of the original data sources in the resulting Knowledge Graph. The provenance information has to include the data provider, temporal information (e.g., data validity), and applied mappings. Often use cases require that only parts of the overall data sources are used. This requires that we use the provenance information and restrict the query access to the Knowledge Graph for a conversation.

6. *Support and drive conversations.* The Knowledge Graph is used to support and guide conversations/dialogs. The first step is to extract facts from the Knowledge Graph and train an NLU engine (e.g., DialogFlow) to understand the user input (entities and intend) in dialogs. The second step is to query the Knowledge Graph to derive the requested user information (e.g., "List all hotels in Seefeld" or "How the weather is on the weekend in Seefeld?"). The Knowledge Graph is also used to guide and drive conversations, e.g., guide the user through a booking process, provide recommendations, or suggest follow-up actions (e.g., booking a hotel room after the user booked an event).

7. *Focus on specific conversational aspects.* Another use case-specific requirement is to focus on a particular aspect or feature for the conversational interfaces. This might be the ability to guide a user through an action by asking for missing required or optional parameters until the action can be completed or providing recommendations or further suggestions.

The pilots that we have introduced in this section have been implemented and used to test and validate the usage of Knowledge Graphs to enable a better understanding of natural language dialogs and knowledge access for touristic chatbots and voice assistants.

4.5   Energy Use Cases

In the *energy domain,* chatbots and Intelligent Personal Assistants powered by Knowledge Graphs are engaging in full conversations with customers of energy companies on various topics related to their products and services. More precisely, the formal knowledge about energy products, tariffs, locations, and services modeled in the Knowledge Graphs is used to extend and enhance the language understanding of Chatbots and Intelligent Personal Assistants. To validate and test our approach in the domain, we are developing several pilots for the largest energy and utility providers in Austria and its regions, such as Wien Energie, Energienetze Steiermark, and Wiener Netze. In the remainder of this section, we are describing the Wien Energie and Energienetze Steiermark pilots.

The Wien Energie[25] pilot is focusing on building and using a Knowledge Graph that captures knowledge about the various products and service variants provided by Wien Energie. Wien Energie has already a chatbot solution in place, developed by us as well, and branded as BotTina, which is available both on Facebook Messenger as well as chatbot widget integrated into the Wien Energie website. By using Knowledge Graphs, we were able to better structure the inner mechanics of the chatbot, reduce the number of intents, and above all improve the quality of the dialogs.

The Wien Energie Knowledge Graph includes information about the electric vehicle charging stations also called EV charging stations in the city of Vienna. To model EV charging stations, we extended the schema.org vocabulary with additional types and properties. Using our extension, it is possible to model information such as the different types of plugs available at an EV charging station, its voltage and power, its address and geo-coordinates, as well as accepted payment methods. We are currently aligning our model with other approaches in the area, e.g., MobiVoc—Open Mobility Vocabulary.[26]

The Knowledge Graph is populated with data received from Wien Energie EV charging station API. The same data is accessible via the online portal Tanke-WienEnergie.[27] The data is then lifted to a semantic representation according to the extended schema.org model we developed and then pushed in the Wien Energie Knowledge Graph. We consider not only static data but dynamic data as well. For example, the number of available plugs, waiting times, and offers is also included in the Knowledge Graph. Using the Knowledge Graph, the chatbot can answer questions such as: "Are there any 11KW Type 2 charging stations around the main station?" or "How many type 2 plugs are available now?" (see Fig. 4.7).

The Wien Energie Knowledge Graph includes also information about the different energy sources that Wien Energie uses to supply its customer. We cover renewable and nonrenewable energy sources from biogas, wind, solar, and hydro energy. Wien Energie offers several products based on such energy sources. All these products, offers, and energy sources are modeled and included in the Wien Energie Knowledge Graph. Using this part of the Knowledge Graph, the Wien Energie chatbot is able to answer complex questions, for instance, "Which tariffs are based on renewable energy sources?" or "Which Gas tariffs have a price guarantee?"

The Energienetze Steiermark[28] pilot is focusing on building and using a Knowledge Graph that captures knowledge about the various products and services provided by the Energienetze Steiermark. It is an Austrian energy and utility supply company. It operates in the fields of electricity, gas, and heat throughout Austria with a focus on the Austrian state of Styria. As in the case of Wien Energie, Energienetze Steiermark has already a chatbot solution in place. Branded as "Herr Ewald," the

---

[25]https://www.wienenergie.at

[26]http://schema.mobivoc.org/

[27]https://www.tanke-wienenergie.at/

[28]https://www.e-netze.at/

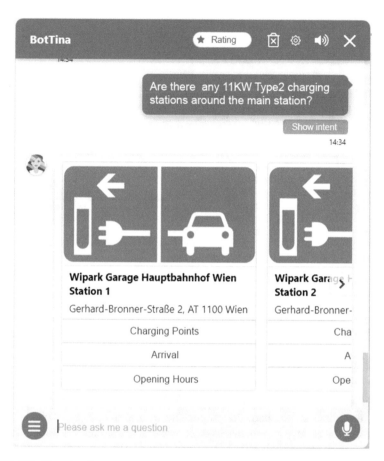

Fig. 4.7 WienEnergie pilot—chatbot answers based on EV charging stations modeled in the Knowledge Graph

chatbot is available on the Energienetze Steiermark website. The focus of this pilot is to model and integrate knowledge about products, energy sources, services, offers, and partners of Energienetze Steiermark and make this knowledge available to power an enhanced version of Herr Ewald chatbot. Figure 4.8 provides an overview of the top-level types introduced to model the domain of Energienetze Steiermark.

A significant part of the Energienetze Steiermark Knowledge Graph includes information about their various products and services. Gas-based heaters, boilers, hot water pumps, and high-, medium-, and low-voltage power networks are just few of the products provided by Energienetze Steiermark and modeled in their Knowledge Graph.

Using the Knowledge Graph, the enhanced version of the chatbot can answer questions such as "Where is the next Bösch partner company?" or "Is there a partner company for Bösch in Leibnitz?"

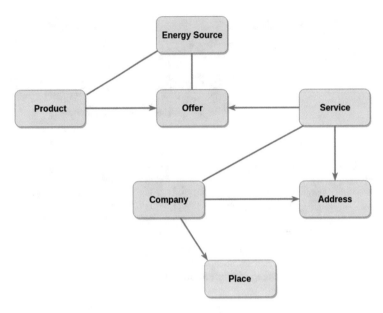

Fig. 4.8 Energienetze Steiermark domain model top-level types

4.6   Further Verticals

The methods and tools for constructing, implementing, and curating Knowledge Graphs described in our book are applicable in a multitude of domains and for various use cases where humans interact with chatbots and Intelligent Personal Assistants through conversational interfaces. In all these use cases, information needs to be extracted from various heterogeneous data sources, brought as knowledge in a machine processable form, reconciled, integrated, and then made accessible through conversational interfaces.

In the *education domain*, institutions such as schools and universities can use Knowledge Graphs to model information about their study programs, the different subjects they teach, and the educational and connected services they offer such as library access and printing. Furthermore, FAQs information can be modeled and integrated, which are then used to power the educational Chatbots and Intelligent Personal Assistants. To validate and test our approach in the educational domain, we are currently developing two pilots, namely:

- *The University of Innsbruck pilot* is focusing on constructing a Knowledge Graph about study programs offered by the University of Innsbruck. The Knowledge Graph is used to improve conversations related to the different study programs, subjects, and examinations. Based on the entities and relations modeled in the Knowledge Graph, dynamic intents are created to query the content from the Knowledge Graph and answer questions such as "Which study programs are offered by the Faculty of Biology?" or "How many semesters do I need to study for the Master's Programme Business Law?"

- *The University of Vienna (UniWien) pilot* has a focus on modeling and integrating internal data sources as well as educational and connected services, such as printing, scanning, charging, and ordering and the usage of terminals. Another main topic is the university cards and their usage for accessing services. The Knowledge Graph is also used to better structure the existing University of Vienna FAQs for different roles, i.e., students, university employees, and external users. The UniWien Chatbot supports question such as "Which services can I use with my ucard?" or "What are the printing costs for a student?"

In the *finance domain,* we develop the Wiener Börse pilot, which focuses on modeling knowledge about companies, equities, bonds, and indexes available on the Vienna Stock Exchange.[29] In particular, this pilot is accessing data in real time. High-frequency data are essential to enable the chatbot and Intelligent Personal Assistant to provide accurate, up-to-date information. The chatbot answers questions such as "What is the stock price of X?" and "Which stocks have lost the most?"

Finally, *retail* is another domain where chatbots and Intelligent Personal Assistants based on Knowledge Graphs will radically change the e-marketing and e-commerce processes. By using natural language, in written or spoken form, customers will be able to search for products that fit their needs and then may buy these products, by directly engaging in natural dialogs with the retail chatbots and Intelligent Personal Assistants. The Wortmann pilot, with a focus on dialog-based access to clothing and footwear products, models and integrates information about product catalogs, product stocks, shops, and connected services into a retail Knowledge Graph for Wortmann Schuh Holding KG.[30] The Knowledge Graph improves the conversations of the existing Wortmann chatbot. More precisely, it is supporting the Wortmann chatbot by answering more complex questions about Wortmann products or e-commerce processes.

4.7 Summary

As evident from the market data regarding conversational AI, chatbots and Intelligent Personal Assistants are on the way to become the main interface for accessing information. However, without knowledge, the capabilities of these conversational agents are limited. In this section, we introduced Onlim, a knowledge-based conversational AI solution. We explained from which aspects Knowledge Graphs can improve conversational interfaces and presented several real-world applications. Our

---

[29]https://www.wienerborse.at/en/ which is one of the oldest and most established exchange in Central, Eastern, and Southeastern Europe.

[30]https://www.wortmann-group.com/de/home, a leading shoe and clothes production and distribution company in Europe.

use cases presented examples from tourism and energy verticals, as well as indications of how our solution can expand to further verticals such as education, finance, and retail. The pilots cover different domains and require methods and tools to cope with a variety of data models, volumes, and velocities integrated into Knowledge Graphs. They provide foundations to validate construction, integration, management, curation, access, and usage of Knowledge Graphs to power chatbots and Intelligent Personal Assistants.

Chapter 5
Conclusions

With this book, we are aiming to provide answers to three essential questions: *what* are Knowledge Graphs, *how* are they built and accessed, and *why* are they important? We elaborated on several possible definitions of Knowledge Graphs and identified as core feature the extremely large amount of interlinked data they try to turn into knowledge. This significantly exceeds any traditional AI approach. We described in detail several approaches for constructing, hosting, curating, and deploying Knowledge Graphs, and we showed their usage for dialog-based information access that revolutionizes information access by humans. We described applications in the areas of e-tourism and beyond.

A severe issue in understanding Knowledge Graphs is the answer to the question of whether they are a new phenomenon or not. On the one hand, *they are not.* Semantic networks arose in the 1960s of the last century as a means to connect pieces of knowledge and founded the area of knowledge representation (Brachman 1990) and knowledge-based systems (Akerkar and Sajja 2010). On the other hand, *they are quite a new phenomenon*, due to the fact that size and focus matters. Traditional KR systems separated the factual and terminological knowledge from each other and put the former in the ABox and the latter into the TBox. The focus was on elaborating the TBox, and usually, the ABox was quite a small set of facts for illustrating the approach. Actually this was, the usual sandbox approach of AI in the 1980s. Knowledge-based systems slightly improved the number of facts in the knowledge base to tens of thousands and in the case of CYC, even to millions (Lenat 1995). Still, the focus was complete, concise, consistent, and correct axioms over these facts and millions look tiny compared with billions and soon trillions of facts captured by an average-sized Knowledge Graph (see Fig. 5.1).

It is not only the size that turns things upside down. Rise in quantity often goes along with changes in quality. With the size comes inherent heterogeneity of the data which inherently makes axioms and constraints on top of them an unfeasible business. Data from different contexts and sources do inherently reflect the different point of views and easily—if not immediately—lead to contradictions when trying to express their meaning by monolithic axioms and rules. Trying to resolve these

© Springer Nature Switzerland AG 2020
D. Fensel et al., *Knowledge Graphs*, https://doi.org/10.1007/978-3-030-37439-6_5

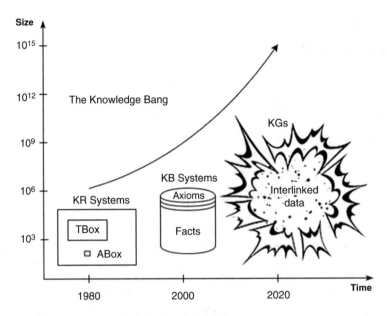

Fig. 5.1 The inflationary growth of the Knowledge Universe

inconsistences at the layer of the interwoven data is neither feasible nor scalable, nor is it the conceptually right approach. Building up meaningful heterogeneous and distributed, domain, and task-specific TBoxes on top of existing Knowledge Graphs looks like a necessary and exciting way to go (e.g., see Töpper et al. 2012; Socher et al. 2013; Galárraga et al. 2013; Galárraga et al. 2015; Paulheim 2018a). One could call them *micro TBoxes* in reference to microtheories of CYC (Guha 1991), however, without the requirement that they are used as a structure for the (semantic) data lake (see Fig. 5.2 and Sect. 3.3).

This layer of domain- and task-specific views is actually the place where interlinked *data are turned into knowledge*. Building up this knowledge access layer based on task-specific problem-solving brings into play a pile of work of the Knowledge Acquisition Workshop Series in Banff, Alberta[1] (see, e.g., Schreiber et al. 1993; Eriksson et al. 1995; Fensel 2000) as a means to build *Knowledge Graph Systems (KGS)*. Modeling and engineering such artifacts call for a new area of science on *knowledge at scale* that may be called *(computational) Knowledge Science*[2] with all its implication on existing educational curricula. It is also the point where traditional AI techniques can come into the game. Large amounts of facts can be enriched and compressed by the elegance of constraints, rules, or axioms, given the specific view that is taken on these data.

---

[1] http://ksi.cpsc.ucalgary.ca/KAW/

[2] Coined by Juan Sequeda, see http://www.juansequeda.com/blog/

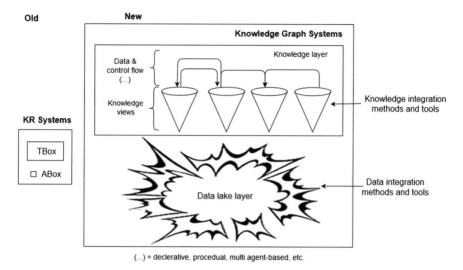

Fig. 5.2 Knowledge Graph System Architecture

In the future, we expect Knowledge Graphs soon to grow to trillions of facts and beyond quickly. Just to mention the frillions of data that soon may be added by the *Internet of Things*.[3] This introduces harsh requirements on methods that can handle them. Even in the optimistic case, Paulheim (2018b) estimates the related costs with billions of dollars. Keeping scale without cost explosion by developing scalable scientific and engineering methods and frameworks is an obvious requirement for the success of the Knowledge Graph System adventure.

---

[3]See the Internet of Things Series by Springer, https://www.springer.com/series/11636

Appendix

Here we provide syntax and semantics of our domain modeling formalism.

A.1 Abstract Syntax and Semantics of Domain Specifications

Domain specification is a process that generates domain-specific patterns by applying an operator to the schema.org vocabulary. Through such patterns, the generic complexity of schema.org is reduced, and its domain specificness is increased. Moreover, it can provide restrictions and constraints to the vocabulary in order to make it suitable for a specific task. The generic complexity of schema.org comes from its wide but shallow coverage of multiple domains and its flexible data model. Domain specification process removes types and properties from the vocabulary and extends it when needed to have a finer-grained coverage of specific domains. By default, the schema.org data model supports properties with global ranges. Domain-specific patterns apply the restrictions on ranges through local properties (i.e., property ranges are defined per domain) for properties. In this appendix, we introduce three different types of domain specification processes. We propose an abstract syntax based on the Shapes Constraint Language (SHACL) (Knublauch and Kontokostas 2017) and the semantics for verification of annotations against domain-specific patterns. This work is based on Şimşek et al. (2019b), where also additional explanations and examples are provided.

© Springer Nature Switzerland AG 2020
D. Fensel et al., *Knowledge Graphs*, https://doi.org/10.1007/978-3-030-37439-6

A.1.1 SHACL (As We Adopt)

SHACL is a recent W3C recommendation for defining constraints over RDF data. The language does not have a normative abstract syntax nor a formal semantics.[1] A syntactically well-formed SHACL shape is ensured by a set of shapes that implement[2] the SHACL Syntax Rules.[3] For the domain specification language, we use a subset of SHACL-CORE[4] elements. In this section, we give a brief introduction to the SHACL elements we adopt for the syntax of our language.

A shape is identified with an IRI or a blank node and fits at least one of the following conditions:

1. A SHACL instance of sh:NodeShape or sh:PropertyShape
2. Subject of a triple that has sh:targetClass, sh:targetNode, sh:targetObjectsOf or sh:targetSubjectsOf as predicate
3. Subject of a triple that has a parameter as a predicate
4. A value of a shape-expecting, non-list-taking parameter such as sh:node
5. A member of a SHACL list that is a value of a shape-expecting and list-taking parameter such as sh:or

SHACL Core Vocabulary defines two different kinds of shapes, namely, node shapes and property shapes. Node shapes target a set of nodes in an RDF data graph. These targeted nodes are called focus nodes. Property shapes target the values of specific properties of focus nodes. Target specifications select the focus nodes in an RDF graph. There are several ways to select a set of focus nodes as the target in SHACL; however, for domain specifications, we are only interested in class-based targets.

A *class-based* target selects a set of nodes in an RDF graph that are instances of the specified class as the value of the property sh:targetClass.

Shapes can define certain constraints on focus nodes and property values. Our constraints are defined by constraint component instances attached to a shape with parameters. In the domain specification language, we are only interested in a subset of the constraint components, namely, value type (sh:class and sh:datatype), cardinality (sh:minCount), shape-based (sh:node and sh:property), and logical constraint components (sh:or).

A *value type* constraint component specifies a constraint on the range of a property for a domain. For our domain specification language, we adopt the sh: class and sh:datatype parameters in order to constrain the type of property value.

---

[1]See https://www.w3.org/TR/shacl-abstract-syntax/ for details and a link to a proposed abstract syntax and semantics. Last accessed on 23.03.2019.

[2]https://www.w3.org/ns/shacl-shacl

[3]https://www.w3.org/TR/shacl/\#syntax-rules

[4]sh prefix is used for SHACL-Core namespace.

A *cardinality constraint* component defines a cardinality constraint on number of values of a given property. We utilize the sh:minCount parameter for minimum cardinality constraints.

A *shape-based* constraint component defines a constraint where the value nodes need to conform to the specified shape. For our domain specification language, we use property shape constraints with sh:property parameter to specify the remaining properties on a type and node shape constraints with sh:node parameter to define local ranges (typically a more restricted version of a type in the global range) for properties of a type.

A *logical constraint* component implements common logical operators AND, OR, NOT, and XOR on a list of shapes. For the domain specification language, we adopt only the OR operator with sh:or parameter for specifying disjunction of value type and node shape constraints.

A.1.2 Conceptual Description of Domain Specification

We define the following types of domain specifications:

- A *Simple Domain Specification* (SDS) generates a Simple Domain Specific Pattern (SDSP) through removing types and properties from the schema.org vocabulary.
- A *Restriction Domain Specification* (RDS) generates a Restricted Domain Specific Pattern (RDSP) by restricting the ranges of the remaining properties of the remaining types in an SDSP.
- An *Extension Domain Specification* (EDS) generates an Extended Domain Specific Pattern (EDSP) by adding new types and properties to an SDSP or RDSP.

In the remainder of this section, we describe these domain specification types and their relationship conceptually. Additionally, we give examples.

A.1.2.1 Simple Domain Specification (SDS)

The SDS generates an SDSP through following steps:

1. Remove types and properties from the schema.org vocabulary.
2. For a remaining type, define local properties from the remaining properties, as a set of (type, property) pairs where property has type in its domain.
3. For each local property on a type, define a range as a set of ((type, property), rangeType) where rangeType is one of the remaining types and in the range of property.[5]

---

[5]As we may exclude some types and given the disjunctive nature of value ranges in schema.org this may already imply a restriction of the range of a property as a side effect.

The following example (see Table A.1) is an SDS operator in SHACL syntax[6] that defines local properties and ranges on schema:Hotel.[7]

A.1.2.2 Restriction Domain Specification

The RDS process deletes a type in the range of a property in an SDSP or replaces it with a subtype and generates an RDSP. The example in Table A.2 is an RDS operator in SHACL syntax that replaces the range of schema:location property on schema:Hotel with a more restricted subtype of schema:PostalAddress.

A.1.2.3 Extension Domain Specification

An EDS process generates an extended domain-specific pattern by extending an SDSP or an RDSP through:

- Adding new types and properties from an external vocabulary
- Defining new properties to an existing type from an external vocabulary
- Adding types from an external vocabulary to the ranges of properties on an existing type

The example in Table A.3 shows an EDS operator in SHACL syntax. It adds a new property, totalNumberOfBeds, to the type schema:Hotel from an external extension of schema.org.

A.1.3 Abstract Syntax

The abstract syntax below specifies how the SHACL components are utilized to define Simple Domain Specification (SDS), Restriction Domain Specification (RDS), and Extension Domain Specification (EDS) operators. We describe the abstract syntax for domain specifications with "EBNF for XML" notation.[8] We extend the notation with the [..] structure for describing special sequences in natural language (e.g., [a valid URI]).

An SDS operator is a node shape that is identified with a URI or a blank node. An SDS operator has a target type from the schema.org vocabulary and contains one or more property shapes, each of which represents the definition of a local property on the target schema.org type.

---

[6]The examples in SHACL syntax replace schema.org datatypes such as Text with XSD datatype such as string for compatibility with existing Semantic Web stack.

[7]*schema* is the prefix for schema.org namespace.

[8]https://www.w3.org/TR/2004/REC-xml-20040204/#sec-notation

Table A.1 An SDS operator in SHACL syntax

```
@prefix sh: <http://www.w3.org/ns/shacl#>.
@prefix schema: <http://schema.org/>.
@prefix ds-tourism: <https://ds.sti2.org/tourism/>.
@prefix xsd: <http://www.w3.org/2001/XMLSchema#>.

  ds-tourism:Hotel a sh:NodeShape;

      sh:property [
          sh:path schema:name;
          sh:datatype xsd:string;
          sh:minCount 1;
      ];
      sh:property [
          sh:path schema:checkInTime;
          sh:datatype xsd:time;
          sh:minCount 1;
      ];
      sh:property [
          sh:path schema:checkOutTime;
          sh:datatype xsd:time;
          sh:minCount 1;
      ];
      sh:property [
          sh:path schema:location;
          sh:class schema:PostalAddress;
          sh:minCount 1;
      ].
```

SDS ::= **NodeShape, SDOTargetType, SDSPropertyShape+;**
NodeShape ::= **Identifier, NodeShapeType;**
Identifier ::= [a URI] | [a BlankNode];
NodeShapeType ::= [URI of the SHACL NodeShape Type];
SDOTargetType ::= [a class-based target whose value is a URI of a schema.org type];

A property shape in an SDS consists of a schema.org property and one or more type specifications for the range of the property. It may also optionally contain a cardinality constraint to specify whether a property is required. A property shape may specify a range with multiple disjunct types.

Table A.2 An RDS operator in SHACL syntax

```
@prefix sh: <http://www.w3.org/ns/shacl#>.
@prefix schema: <http://schema.org/>.
@prefix ds-tourism: <https://ds.sti2.org/tourism/>.
@prefix xsd: <http://www.w3.org/2001/XMLSchema#>.

ds-tourism:Hotel a sh:NodeShape;

    sh:property [

        sh:path schema:name;

         sh:datatype xsd:string;

        sh:minCount 1;

    ];

    sh:property [

        sh:path schema:checkInTime;

         sh:datatype xsd:time;

        sh:minCount 1;

    ];

    sh:property [

        sh:path schema:checkOutTime;

         sh:datatype xsd:time;

        sh:minCount 1;

    ];

    sh:property [

        sh:path schema:location;

        sh:class schema:PostalAddress;

        sh:minCount 1;

        sh:node [

                a sh:NodeShape;

                sh:property [

                    sh:path schema:addressCountry;

                    sh:datatype xsd:string;

                    sh:minCount 1;
```

(continued)

Table A.2 (continued)

```
                    ];

            sh:property [

                    sh:path schema:addressLocality;

                    sh:datatype xsd:string;

                    sh:minCount 1;

            ];

    ]

].
```

SDSPropertyShape ::= **SDOProperty, MinCount?, (ValueTypeConstraint+ | SimpleDisjunctiveConstraint);**
SDOProperty ::= [URI of a schema.org property];

A value type constraint enforces the type of a value. It requires the URI of a type in schema.org vocabulary as the value of sh:class parameter or the URI of an XSD datatype as the value of sh:datatype property.

ValueTypeConstraint ::= **SimpleClassConstraint | DatatypeConstraint ;**
SimpleClassConstraint ::= [A SHACL Class constraint with sh:class parameter and a value t where t is a schema.org type that is more specific than schema: Thing];
DatatypeConstraint ::= [A SHACL Datatype constraint with sh:datatype parameter and a value t where t is a schema.org datatype];

A cardinality constraint enforces the number of values a property can take. It takes only the integer 1 as value for sh:minCount parameters to specify minimum required value occurrences.

MinCount ::= [minimum cardinality constraint with sh:minCount 1];

A simple disjunctive constraint applies logical OR operation to a given list of value type constraints.

SimpleDisjunctiveConstraint ::= [OR(**ValueTypeConstraint+**)] ;

An RDS is a SHACL node shape with a target type from the schema.org vocabulary and one or more property shapes.

RDS ::= **NodeShape, SDOTargetType, RDSPropertyShape+;**

A property shape in an RDS extends a property shape in SDS with range constraints.

Table A.3 An EDS operator in SHACL syntax

```
@prefix sh: <http://www.w3.org/ns/shacl#>.
@prefix schema: <http://schema.org/>.
@prefix ds-tourism: <https://ds.sti2.org/tourism/>.
@prefix xsd: <http://www.w3.org/2001/XMLSchema#>.
@prefix schema-tourism: <https://schema-tourism.sti2.org/ns/>

ds-tourism:Hotel a sh:NodeShape;

    sh:property [

        sh:path schema:name;

         sh:datatype xsd:string;

        sh:minCount 1;

    ];

    sh:property [

        sh:path schema:checkInTime;

         sh:datatype xsd:time;

         sh:minCount 1;

    ];

    sh:property [

        sh:path schema:checkOutTime;

         sh:datatype xsd:time;

        sh:minCount 1;

    ];

    sh:property [

        sh:path schema-tourism:totalNumberOfBeds;

         sh:datatype xsd:positiveInteger;

    ];

    sh:property [

        sh:path schema:location;

        sh:class schema:PostalAddress;

        sh:minCount 1;

        sh:node [
```

(continued)

Table A.3 (continued)

```
              a sh:NodeShape;

              sh:property [

                  sh:path schema:addressCountry;

                  sh:datatype xsd:string;

                  sh:minCount 1;

              ];

              sh:property [

                  sh:path schema:addressLocality;

                  sh:datatype xsd:string;

                  sh:minCount 1;

              ];

          ]

      ].
```

RDSPropertyShape ::= **SDOProperty, MinCount?, (ValueTypeConstraint | RangeConstraint | DisjunctiveConstraint)+;**

A range constraint consists of a value type constraint that declares a type in the range and a node constraint that further constrains the specified type.

RangeConstraint ::= **ValueTypeConstraint, NodeConstraint;**
NodeConstraint ::= **NodeShape, RDSPropertyShape+;**

A disjunctive constraint extends a simple disjunctive constraint in an SDS by applying logical OR operator on a list of value type constraints and range restrictions.

DisjunctiveConstraint ::= **[OR{(ValueTypeConstraint | RangeConstraint)+}] ;**

An EDS operator extends an SDS or an RDS operators with types from an external vocabulary.

EDS ::= **NodeShape, (SDOTargetType | ExtTargetType), EDSPropertyShape+;**
ExtTargetType ::= **[URI of type t where t ∈ Text];**
EDSPropertyShape ::= **(SDOProperty | ExtProperty), MinCount?, (ExtValueTypeConstraint | ExtRangeConstraint | ExtDisjunctiveConstraint)+;**

ExtProperty ::= [URI of property p where p ∈ Pext];
ExtValueTypeConstraint ::= **SimpleClassConstraint** | **ExtClassConstraint** |
  DatatypeConstraint; ExtClassConstraint ::= [A SHACL Class constraint
  with a value t is a type from an external vocabulary];
ExtRangeConstraint ::= **ExtValueTypeConstraint, ExtNodeConstraint;**
ExtNodeConstraint ::= **NodeShape, EDSPropertyShape+;**
ExtDisjunctiveConstraint ::= [OR{(**ExtValueTypeConstraint** | **ExtRan**
  geConstraint)+}]

In SHACL syntax, an EDS operator can be seen as an SDS and RDS operator
with types or properties from a namespace other than schema.org. There are no
syntactic extensions for SHACL needed to define these operators. Therefore, a
domain specification operator is also a valid SHACL shape and can be used by
existing SHACL tools.

A.1.4 Semantics

An annotation can be verified against a domain-specific pattern that is generated by a
domain specification operator. The verification is done by checking an annotation
against the constraints defined by a domain specification operator. We define two
predicates, namely, *applies* and *verifies*, in order to explain the semantics of domain-
specific patterns and annotation verification.[9]
A domain-specific pattern applies to an annotation when the target type of the
domain specification operator that produces the pattern is the same type as the root
type of the annotation.

- *dso* is a domain specification operator that generates a domain-specific pattern.
  anno is an annotation that is a directed graph with exactly one source node
  (sn) that has no incoming edges. An annotation consists of a source node (sn),
  other nodes ($n_1 . . . n_i$) that are reachable through at least one path from the source
  node, and labeled edges $e_1 . . . e_i$. The nodes represent instances of types from
  schema.org or an extension of schema.org. The edges are properties from schema.
  org or an extension of schema.org. For any directed edge (e) in anno, e.from
  represents the source node while e.to represents the target node.

  Formally, applies (dso, anno) holds true when:

- isElementOf (sn, t) holds true where t is the value of **SDOTargetType** in dso

---

[9]The semantics is described with SDS and RDS operator components from the abstract syntax.
Replacing them with EDS operator components is rather trivial.

An annotation is verified, when it conforms to a domain specification operator that applies to it. For anno and dso pair that make *applies* (dso, anno) true, the predicate *verifies* (dso, anno) holds true, iff:

- Given that oe in anno is a directed edge from sn to n, for each oe, there exists a property shape (ps) in dso and *satisfies* (oe, ps) holds true.
- There exists at least one oe, for each ps with a **MinCount**.

satisfies (oe, ps) holds true iff:

- The label of oe is the same as the value of **SDOProperty** in ps.
- For each **ValueTypeConstraint**, **NodeConstraint**, and **DisjunctiveConstraint** (cons) in ps,[10] *satisfiesRangeRestriction* (oe.to, cons) holds true.

satisfiesRangeRestriction (n, cons) holds true iff:

- If cons is a **ValueTypeConstraint** then:

  – isElementOf (n, t_a) and isA(t_a, t_b) and t_b is equal to the value of ValueTypeConstraint.

- If cons is a **NodeConstraint** then:

  – Given that oen is a directed edge from n to n_2, for each oen, there exists a property shape (psnc) in cons.
  – There exists at least one oen for each psnc with a **MinCount**.
  – isElementOf (n, t_c) and isA (t_c, t_d) and t_d is equal to the value of **ValueTypeConstraint** in cons.
  – satisfies (oen.to, psnc) holds true.

- If cons is a **DisjunctiveConstraint:**

  – For the list of constraints (c_1 ... c_n) in cons, satisfies (n, c_1) V satisfies(n, c_2) V satisfies(n, c_3) ... V satisfies(n, c_4) holds true.

---

[10]Multiple constraints are treated as conjunction.

References

M. Achichi, Z. Bellahsene, K. Todorov, Legato results for OAEI 2017, in *Proceedings of the 12th International Workshop on Ontology Matching (OM2017) Co-Located with the 16th International Semantic Web Conference (ISWC2017), CEUR Workshop Proceedings*, vol. 2032, Vienna, Austria, 21 October 2017

M. Acosta, A. Zaveri, E. Simperl, D. Kontokostas, S. Auer, J. Lehmann, Crowdsourcing linked data quality assessment, in *Proceedings of the 12th International Semantic Web Conference (ISWC2013)*, Sydney, Australia, 21–25 October 2013. Springer LNCS, vol. 8219

R. Akerkar, P. Sajja, *Knowledge-Based Systems* (Jones & Bartlett, Sudbury, MA, 2010)

R. Angles, C. Gutiérrez, Querying RDF data from a graph database perspective, in *Proceedings of the 2nd European Semantic Web Conference (ESWC2005)*, Heraklion, Greece, 29 May–1 June 2005. Springer LNCS, vol. 3532

R. Angles, C. Gutiérrez, Survey of graph database models. ACM Comput. Surv. **40**(1), 1–39 (2008)

A. Ankolekar, M. Burstein, J.R. Hobbs, O. Lassila, D. Martin, D. McDermott, S.A. McIlraith, S. Narayanan, M. Paolucci, T. Payne, K. Sycara, DAML-S: web service description for the Semantic Web, in *Proceedings of the 1st International Semantic Web Conference (ISWC2002)*, Sardinia, Italia, 9–12 June 2002. Springer LNCS, vol. 2342

A.P. Aprosio, C. Giuliano, A. Lavelli, Automatic expansion of DBpedia exploiting Wikipedia cross-language information, in *Proceedings of the 10th International Extended Semantic Web Conference (ESWC2013) on the Semantic Web: Semantics and Big Data*, Montpellier, France, 26–30 May 2013. Springer LNCS, vol. 7882

S. Araújo, J. Hidders, D. Schwabe, A.P. de Vries, SERIMI—resource description similarity, RDF instance matching and interlinking, in *Proceedings of the 6th International Workshop on Ontology Matching (OM2011), CEUR Workshop Proceedings*, vol. 814, Bonn, Germany, 24 October 2011

S. Athanasiou, G. Giannopoulos, D. Graux, N. Karagiannakis, J. Lehmann, A.N. Ngomo, K. Patroumpas, M.A. Sherif, D. Skoutas, Big POI data integration with linked data technologies, in *Proceedings of the 22nd International Conference on Extending Database Technology (EDBT2019)*, Lisbon, Portugal, 26–29 March 2019a. OpenProceedings.org

S. Athanasiou, M. Alexakis, G. Giannopoulos, N. Karagiannakis, Y. Kouvaras, P. Mitropoulos, K. Patroumpas, D. Skoutas, SLIPO: large-scale data integration for points of interest, in *Proceedings of the 22nd International Conference on Extending Database Technology (EDBT)*, Lisbon, Portugal, 26–29 March 2019b, pp. 574–577

S. Auer, C. Bizer, G. Kobilarov, J. Lehmann, R. Cyganiak, Z.G. Ives, DBpedia: a nucleus for a web of open data, in *Proceedings of the 6th International Semantic Web Conference (ISWC2007)*,

2nd Asian Semantic Web Conference, (ASWC2007), Busan, Korea, 11–15 November 2007. Springer LNCS, vol. 4825

F. Baader, I. Horrocks, C. Lutz, U. Sattler, *An Introduction to Description Logic* (Cambridge University Press, Cambridge, 2017)

F. Bancilhon, D. Maier, Y. Sagiv, J.D. Ullman, Magic sets and other strange ways to implement logic programs (extended abstract), in *Proceedings of the 5th ACM SIGACT-SIGMOD Symposium on Principles of Database Systems (PODS1986)*, 24–26 March 1986 (ACM, Cambridge)

C. Batini, M. Scannapieco, *Data Quality: Concepts, Methodologies and Techniques. Data-Centric Systems and Applications* (Springer, New York, 2006)

C. Batini, M. Lenzerini, S.B. Navathe, A comparative analysis of methodologies for database schema integration. ACM Comput. Surv. **18**(4), 323–364 (1986)

C. Batini, C. Cappiello, C. Francalanci, A. Maurino, Methodologies for data quality assessment and improvement. ACM Comput. Surv. **41**(3), 1–52 (2009)

S. Battle, A. Bernstein, H. Boley, B. Grosof, M. Gruninger, R. Hull, M. Kifer, D. Martin, S. McIlraith, D. McGuinness, J. Su, S. Tabet, Semantic Web Services Framework (SWSF) overview, W3C member submission (2005). https://www.w3.org/Submission/SWSF/

W. Beek, L. Rietveld, H.R. Bazoobandi, J. Wielemaker, S. Schlobach, LOD laundromat: a uniform way of publishing other people's dirty data, in *Proceedings of the 13th International Semantic Web Conference (ISWC2014)*, Riva del Garda, Italy, 19–23 October 2014. Springer LNCS, vol. 8796

O. Benjelloun, H. Garcia-Molina, D. Menestrina, Q. Su, S.E. Whang, J. Widom, Swoosh: a generic approach to entity resolution. Int. J. Very Large Data Bases **18**(1), 255–276 (2009)

M.K. Bergman, *A Knowledge Representation Practionary—Guidelines Based on Charles Sanders Peirce* (Springer, Cham, 2018)

T. Berners-Lee, D. Connolly, Notation3 (N3): a readable RDF syntax, W3C Team Submission, 14 January 2008. https://www.w3.org/TeamSubmission/2008/SUBM-n3-20080114/

T. Berners-Lee, J. Hendler, O. Lassila, The Semantic Web. Sci. Am. **284**(5), 28–37 (2001)

I. Bhattacharya, L. Getoor, Collective entity resolution in relational data. ACM Trans. Knowl. Discov. Data **1**(1), 5 (2007)

A. Bilke, J. Bleiholder, C. Böhm, K. Draba, F. Naumann, M. Weis, Automatic data fusion with HumMer, in *Proceedings of the 31st International Conference on Very Large Data Bases (VLDB2005)*, VLDB Endowment, Trondheim, Norway, 30 August–2 September 2005

C. Bizer, R. Cygania, Quality-driven information filtering using the WIQA policy framework. J. Web Semant. **7**(1), 1–10 (2009)

C. Bizer, T. Heath, K. Idehen, T. Berners-Lee, Linked data on the web (LDOW2008), in *Proceedings of the 17th International Conference on World Wide Web (WWW2008): Workshop*, 21–25 April 2008 (ACM, Beijing)

C. Bizer, T. Heath, T. Berners-Lee, Linked data—the story so far. Int. J. Semant. Web Inf. Syst. **5**(3), 1–22 (2009)

R. Blanco, B.B. Cambazoglu, P. Mika, N. Torzec, Entity recommendations in web search, in *Proceedings of the 12th International Semantic Web Conference (ISWC2013)*, Sydney, Australia, 21–25 October 2013. Springer LNCS, vol. 8219

J. Bleiholder, F. Naumann, Declarative data fusion—syntax, semantics, and implementation, in *Proceedings of the 9th East European Conference on Advances in Databases and Information Systems (ADBIS2005)*, Tallinn, Estonia, 12–15 September 2005. Springer LNCS, vol. 3631

J. Bleiholder, F. Naumann, Data fusion. ACM Comput. Surv. **41**(1), 1–41 (2009)

J. Bleiholder, K. Draba, F. Naumann, FuSem—exploring different semantics of data fusion, in *Proceedings of the 33rd International Conference on Very Large Data Bases (VLDB2007)*, VLDB Endowment, Vienna, Austria, 23–27 September 2007

K.D. Bollacker, C. Evans, P. Paritosh, T. Sturge, J. Taylor, Freebase: a collaboratively created graph database for structuring human knowledge, in *Proceedings of the 2008 ACM SIGMOD International Conference on Management of Data (SIGMOD2008)*, 09–12 June 2008 (ACM, Vancouver)

P.A. Bonatti, S. Decker, A. Polleres, V. Presutti, Knowledge graphs: new directions for knowledge representation on the Semantic Web (dagstuhl seminar 18371). Dagstuhl Rep. **8**(9), 29–111 (2019)

A. Borodin, G.O. Roberts, J.S. Rosenthal, P. Tsaparas, Link analysis ranking: algorithms, theory, and experiments. ACM Trans. Internet Technol. **5**(1), 231–297 (2005)

R.J. Brachman, On the epistemological status of semantic networks, in *Associative Networks: Representation and Use of Knowledge by Computers*, ed. by N. V. Findler, (Academic, New York, 1979)

R.J. Brachman, The future of knowledge representation, in *Proceedings of the 8th National Conference on Artificial Intelligence (AAAI1990)*, 29 July–3 August 1990 (AAAI Press, Boston)

R.J. Brachman, J.G. Schmolze, An overview of the KL-ONE knowledge representation system. Cogn. Sci. **9**(2), 171–202 (1985)

W.M. Campbell, L. Li, C.K. Dagli, J. Acevedo-Aviles, K. Geyer, J.P. Campbell, C. Priebe, *Cross-Domain Entity Resolution in Social Media*, Technical Report, *arXiv preprint*, 1608.01386 (2016). https://arxiv.org/abs/1608.01386

A. Carlson, J. Betteridge, B. Kisiel, B. Settles, E.R. Hruschka, T.M. Mitchell, Toward an architecture for never-ending language learning, in *Proceedings of the 24th Conference on Artificial Intelligence (AAAI2010)*, 11–15 July 2010 (AAAI Press, Atlanta)

C. Chang, M. Kayed, M.R. Girgis, K.F. Shaalan, A survey of web information extraction systems. IEEE Trans. Knowl. Data Eng. **18**(10), 1411–1428 (2006)

H. Chen, H. Ji, L. Sun, H. Wang, T. Qian, T. Ruan (eds.), *Knowledge Graph and Semantic Computing: Semantic, Knowledge, and Linked Big Data—First China Conference, CCKS 2016, Beijing, China, 19–22 September 2016*. Revised Selected Papers, Springer Communications in Computer and Information Science, vol. 650 (2016)

H. Chen, X. Liu, D. Yin, J. Tang, A survey on dialogue systems: recent advances and new frontiers. ACM SIGKDD Explor. Newsl. **19**(2), 25–35 (2017)

V. Christophides, V. Efthymiou, K. Stefanidis, *Entity Resolution in the Web of Data* (Morgan & Claypool, San Rafael, 2015)

X. Chu, M. Ouzzani, J. Morcos, I.F. Ilyas, P. Papotti, N. Tang, Y. Ye, KATARA: reliable data cleaning with knowledge bases and crowdsourcing, in *Proceedings of the 41st International Conference on Very Large Data Bases (PVLDB2015)*, Hawaii, 31 August–4 September 2015, *VLDB Endowment*, **8**(12), 1952–1955 (2015)

P. Cimiano, S. Handschuh, S. Staab, Towards the self-annotating web, in *Proceedings of the 13th International Conference on World Wide Web (WWW2004)*, 17–20 May 2004 (ACM, New York)

W.J. Clancey, Heuristic classification. Artif. Intell. **27**(3), 289–350 (1985)

E.F. Codd, A relational model of data for large shared data banks. Commun. ACM **13**(6), 377–387 (1970)

M. Croitoru, P. Marquis, S. Rudolph, G. Stapleton (eds.), *Proceedings of the 5th International Workshop on Graph Structures for Knowledge Representation and Reasoning (GKR2017): Revised Selected Papers*, Melbourne, 21 August 2017. Springer LNCS, vol. 10775 (2018)

C. d'Amato, M. Theobald (eds.), *Proceedings of the 14th International Summer School 2018: Reasoning Web. Learning, Uncertainty, Streaming, and Scalability: Tutorial Lectures*, Esch-sur-Alzette, Luxembourg, 22–26 September 2018. Springer LNCS, vol. 11078

V. D'Silva, D. Kroening, G. Weissenbacher, A survey of automated techniques for formal software verification. IEEE Trans. Comput. Aided Des. Integr. Circuits Syst. **27**(7), 1165–1178 (2008)

C. Day, *Record Linkage I: Evaluation of Commercially Available Record Linkage Software for Use in NASS*. US Department of Agriculture, National Agricultural Statistics Service, Research Division (1995)

J. De Bruijn, R. Lara, A. Polleres, D. Fensel, OWL DL vs. OWL flight: conceptual modeling and reasoning for the Semantic Web, in *Proceedings of the 14th International World Wide Web Conference (ISWC2005)*, 10–14 May 2005 (ACM, Chiba, Japan)

G. De Melo, Not quite the same: identity constraints for the web of linked data, in *Proceedings of the 27th Conference on Artificial Intelligence (AAAI2013)*, 14–18 July 2013 (AAAI Press, Bellevue, USA)

J. Debattista, S. Auer, C. Lange, Luzzu—a methodology and framework for linked data quality assessment. J. Data Inf. Qual. **8**(1), 1–32 (2016a)

J. Debattista, C. Lange, S. Auer, A preliminary investigation towards improving linked data quality using distance-based outlier detection, in *Proceedings of the 6th Joint International Semantic Technology Conference (JIST2016): Revised Selected Papers*, Singapore, 2–4 November 2016b. Springer LNCS, vol. 10055

S. Decker, S. Melnik, F. van Harmelen, D. Fensel, M.C.A. Klein, J. Broekstra, M. Erdmann, I. Horrocks, The Semantic Web: the roles of XML and RDF. IEEE Internet Comput. **4**(5), 63–74 (2000)

D. Dell'Aglio, E.D. Valle, F. van Harmelen, A. Bernstein, Stream reasoning: a survey and outlook. Data Sci. **1**(1–2), 59–83 (2017)

M. Dezani-Ciancaglini, R. Horne, V. Sassone, Tracing where and who provenance in linked data: a calculus. Theor. Comput. Sci. **464**, 113–129 (2012)

D. Diefenbach, V. López, K.D. Singh, P. Maret, Core techniques of question answering systems over knowledge bases: a survey. Knowl. Inf. Syst. **55**(3), 529–569 (2018a)

D. Diefenbach, K.D. Singh, P. Maret, WDAqua-core1: a question answering service for RDF knowledge bases, in *Companion Proceedings of the Web Conference (WWW2018)*, 23–27 April 2018b (ACM, Lyon)

D. Dietrich, J. Gray, T. McNamara, A. Poikola, P. Pollock, J. Tait, T. Zijlstra, *Open data handbook* (Open Knowledge International, Cambridge, 2009)

A. Dimou, M.V. Sande, P. Colpaert, R. Verborgh, E. Mannens, R.V. de Walle, RML: a generic language for integrated RDF mappings of heterogeneous data, in *Proceedings of the Workshop on Linked Data on the Web (LDOW2014) Co-Located with the 23rd International World Wide Web Conference (WWW2014), CEUR Workshop Proceedings*, vol. 1184, Seoul, Korea, 8 April 2014

L. Ding, P. Kolari, Z. Ding, S. Avancha, Using ontologies in the Semantic Web: a survey. Ontol. Integr. Ser. Inf. Syst. **14**, 79–113 (2007)

X.L. Dong, F. Naumann, Data fusion—resolving data conflicts for integration. Proc. Very Large Data Bases Endow. **2**(2), 1654–1655 (2009)

X.L. Dong, D. Srivastava, Knowledge curation and knowledge fusion: challenges, models and applications, in *Proceedings of the 2015 ACM International Conference on Management of Data (SIGMOD2015)*, 31 May–4 June 2015 (ACM, Melbourne)

X.L. Dong, L. Berti-Équille, D. Srivastava, Integrating conflicting data: the role of source dependence. Proc. Very Large Data Bases Endow. **2**(1), 550–561 (2009a)

X.L. Dong, L. Berti-Équille, D. Srivastava, Truth discovery and copying detection in a dynamic world. Proc. Very Large Data Bases Endow. **2**(1), 562–573 (2009b)

X.L. Dong, E. Gabrilovich, G. Heitz, W. Horn, N. Lao, K. Murphy, T. Strohmann, S. Sun, W. Zhang, Knowledge vault: a web-scale approach to probabilistic knowledge fusion, in *Proceedings of the 20th ACM Conference on Knowledge Discovery and Data Mining (KDD2014)*, 24–27 August 2014a (ACM, New York)

X.L. Dong, E. Gabrilovich, G. Heitz, W. Horn, K. Murphy, S. Sun, W. Zhang, From data fusion to knowledge fusion. Proc. Very Large Data Bases Endow. **7**(10), 881–892 (2014b)

H.L. Dunn, Record linkage. Am. J. Public Health Nations Health **36**(12), 1412–1416 (1946)

H. Ehrig, C. Ermel, U. Golas, F. Hermann, *Graph and Model Transformation: General Framework and Applications* (Springer, Berlin, 2015)

L. Ehrlinger, W. Wöß, Towards a definition of knowledge graphs, in *Proceedings of the 12th International Conference on Semantic Systems (SEMANTICS2016): Posters and Demos Track, CEUR Workshop Proceedings*, vol. 1695, Leipzig, Germany, 12–15 September 2016

H. Eriksson, Y. Sahar, S.W. Tu, A.R. Puerta, M.A. Musen, Task modeling with reusable problem-solving methods. Artif. Intell. **79**(2), 293–326 (1995)

F. Erxleben, M. Günther, M. Krötzsch, J. Mendez, D. Vrandečić, Introducing wikidata to the linked data web, in *Proceedings of the 13th International Semantic Web Conference (ISWC 2014)*, Riva del Garda, Italy, 19–23 October 2014. Springer LNCS, vol. 8796

D. Esteves, A. Rula, A.J. Reddy, J. Lehmann, Toward veracity assessment in RDF knowledge bases: an exploratory analysis. ACM J. Data Inf. Qual. **9**(3), 1–26 (2018)

M. Färber, F. Bartscherer, C. Menne, A. Rettinger, Linked data quality of DBpedia, Freebase, OpenCyc, Wikidata, and YAGO. Semant. Web J. **9**(1), 77–129 (2018)

D.C. Faye, O. Curé, G. Blin, A survey of RDF storage approaches. Rev. Afr. Rech. Inf. Math. Appl. **15**, 11–35 (2012)

E.A. Feigenbaum, Knowledge engineering: the applied side of artificial intelligence. Ann. NY Acad. Sci. **426**(1), 91–107 (1984). (Originally published 1980)

D. Fensel, *Problem-Solving Methods: Understanding, Description, Development, and Reuse.* Springer LNAI, vol. 1791 (2000)

D. Fensel, C. Bussler, The web service modeling framework WSMF. Electron. Commer. Res. Appl. **1**(2), 113–137 (2002)

D. Fensel, M.A. Musen, The Semantic Web: a brain for humankind. IEEE Intell. Syst. **16**(2), 24–25 (2001)

D. Fensel, F. van Harmelen, Unifying reasoning and search to web scale. IEEE Internet Comput. **11**(2), 94–96 (2007)

D. Fensel, M. Erdmann, R. Studer, Ontology groups: semantically enriched subnets of the WWW, in *Proceedings of the 1st International Workshop Intelligent Information Integration During the 21st German Annual Conference on Artificial Intelligence*, Freiburg, Germany, September 1997

D. Fensel, J. Angele, S. Decker, M. Erdmann, H. Schnurr, R. Studer, A. Witt, Lessons learned from applying AI to the web. Int. J. Coop. Inf. Syst. **9**(4), 361–382 (2000)

D. Fensel, F. van Harmelen, B. Andersson, P. Brennan, H. Cunningham, E.D. Valle, F. Fischer, Z. Huang, A. Kiryakov, T.K. Lee, L. Schooler, V. Tresp, S. Wesner, M.J. Witbrock, N. Zhong, Towards LarKC: a platform for web-scale reasoning, in *Proceedings of the 2nd International Conference on Semantic Computing (ICSC2008)*, 4–7 August 2008 (IEEE Computer Society, Santa Clara)

J.D. Fernández, W. Beek, M.A. Martínez-Prieto, M. Arias. LOD-a-lot: a queryable dump of the LOD cloud, in *Proceedings of the 16th International Semantic Web Conference (ISWC2017)*, Vienna, Austria, 21–25 October 2017. Springer LNCS, vol. 10588

Ó. Ferrández, C. Spurk, M. Kouylekov, I. Dornescu, S. Ferrández, M. Negri, R. Izquierdo, D. Tomás, C. Orasan, G. Neumann, B. Magnini, J.L.V. González, The QALL-ME framework: a specifiable-domain multilingual question answering architecture. J. Web Semant. **9**(2), 137–145 (2011)

D. Fleischhacker, H. Paulheim, V. Bryl, J. Völker, C. Bizer, Detecting errors in numerical linked data using cross-checked outlier detection, in *Proceedings of the 13th International Conference on Management of Data (ISWC2014)*, Riva del Garda, Italy, 19–23 October 2014. Springer LNCS, vol. 8796

A. Flemming, *Qualitätsmerkmale von Linked Data-veröffentlichenden Daten-quellen*, Diploma thesis, Humboldt-Universität zu Berlin, 2011

C. Fürber, M. Hepp, Using SPARQL and SPIN for data quality management on the Semantic Web, in *Proceedings of the 13th International Conference on Business Information Systems (BIS2010)*, Berlin, Germany, 3–5 May 2010a. Springer LNBI, vol. 47

C. Fürber, M. Hepp, Using Semantic Web resources for data quality management, in *Proceedings of the 17th International Conference on Knowledge Engineering and Management by the Masses (EKAW2010)*, Lisbon, Portugal, 11–15 October 2010b. Springer LNCS, vol. 6317

C. Fürber, M. Hepp, SWIQA—a Semantic Web information quality assessment framework, in *Proceedings of the 19th European Conference on Information Systems (ECIS2011)*, Association for Information Systems (AIS eLibrary), Helsinki, Finland, 9–11 June 2011

A. Fuxman, E. Fazli, R.J. Miller, ConQuer: efficient management of inconsistent databases, in *Proceedings of the International Conference on Management of Data (SIGMOD2005)*, 14–16 June 2005 (ACM, Baltimore)

L.A. Galárraga, C. Teflioudi, K. Hose, F.M. Suchanek, AMIE: association rule mining under incomplete evidence in ontological knowledge bases, in *Proceedings of the 22nd International Conference on the World Wide Web (WWW2013)*, 13–17 May 2013 (ACM, Rio de Janeiro)

L. Galárraga, C. Teflioudi, K. Hose, F.M. Suchanek, Fast rule mining in ontological knowledge bases with AMIE+. Int. J. Very Large Data Bases **24**(6), 707–730 (2015)

E. Gamma, R. Helm, R. Johnson, J. Vlissides, *Design Patterns: Elements of Reusable Object-Oriented Software* (Addison-Wesley Longman, Boston, MA, 1995)

A. Gangemi, A.G. Nuzzolese, V. Presutti, F. Draicchio, A. Musetti, P. Ciancarini, Automatic typing of DBpedia entities, in *Proceedings of the 11th International Semantic Web Conference (ISWC2012)*, Boston, 11–15 November 2012. Springer LNCS, vol. 7649

H. Garcia-Molina, J.D. Ullman, J. Widom, *Database Systems: The Complete Book, Chapter 7*, 2nd edn. (Pearson International Editing, 2009)

L.M. Garshol, A. Borge, Hafslund Sesam—an archive on semantics, in *Proceedings of the 10th Extending Semantic Web Conference (ESWC2013): Semantics and Big Data*, Montpellier, France, 26–30 May 2013. Springer LNCS, vol. 7882

G. Gawriljuk, A. Harth, C.A. Knoblock, P.A. Szekely, A scalable approach to incrementally building knowledge graphs, in *Proceedings of the 20th International Conference on Theory and Practice of Digital Libraries (TPDL2016)*, Hannover, Germany, 5–9 September 2016. Springer LNCS, vol. 9819

M.R. Genesereth, A.M. Keller, O.M. Duschka, Infomaster: an information integration system, in *Proceedings of the International Conference on Management of Data (SIGMOD1997)*, 13–15 May 1997 (ACM Press, Tucson)

L. Getoor, A. Machanavajjhala, Entity resolution: theory, practice & open challenges, in *Proceedings of the 38th International Conference on Very Large Data Bases (VLDB2012)*, **5**(12), 2018–2019 (2012)

L. Getoor, A. Machanavajjhala, Entity resolution for big data, in *Proceedings of the 19th International Conference on Knowledge Discovery and Data Mining (KDD2013): Tutorial*, 11–14 August 2013 (ACM, Chicago)

G. Giannopoulos, D. Skoutas, T. Maroulis, N. Karagiannakis, S. Athanasiou, FAGI: a framework for fusing geospatial RDF data, in *Proceedings of the Confederated International Conferences on the Move to Meaningful Internet Systems (OTM2014)*, Amantea, Italy, 27–31 October 2014. Springer LNCS, vol. 8841

J.M. Giménez-García, M.C. Duarte, A. Zimmermann, C. Gravier, E.R. Hruschka Jr., P. Maret, *NELL2RDF: Reading the Web, and Publishing It as Linked Data*, Technical Report (2018). https://arxiv.org/abs/1804.05639

H. Glaser, I. Millard, W. Sung, S. Lee, P. Kim, B. You, Research on linked data and co-reference resolution, in *Proceedings of the International Conference on Dublin Core and Metadata Applications (DCMI2019)*, Dublin Core Metadata Initiative, Seoul, Korea, 12–16 October 2009

A. Gómez-Pérez, M. Fernandez-Lopez, O. Corcho, *Ontological Engineering: With Examples from the Areas of Knowledge Management, e-Commerce and the Semantic Web* (Springer, Berlin, 2010)

J.M. Gómez-Pérez, J.Z. Pan, G. Vetere, H. Wu, Enterprise knowledge graph: an introduction, in *Exploiting Linked Data and Knowledge Graphs in Large Organisations*, ed. by J. Z. Pan, G. Vetere, J. M. Gómez-Pérez, H. Wu, (Springer, Cham, 2017)

M. González Bermúdez, *DIGUI: A Flexible Dialogue System for Guiding the User Interaction to Access Web Services*, Ph.D. thesis, Universitat Politècnica de Catalunya, 2010

I.J. Goodfellow, Y. Bengio, A.C. Courville, *Deep Learning. Adaptive Computation and Machine Learning* (MIT Press, Cambridge, 2016)

P. Groth, F. van Harmelen, A.-C. Ngonga-Ngomo, V. Presutti, J.F. Sequeda, M. Dumontier, Grand challenges, ed. by P.A. Bonatti, S. Decker, A. Polleres, V. Presutti, in *Knowledge Graphs: New*

Directions for Knowledge Representation on the Semantic Web (Dagstuhl Seminar 18371), Dagstuhl Rep. **8**(9), 29–111 (2019)

C. Guéret, P.T. Groth, C. Stadler, J. Lehmann, Assessing linked data mappings using network measures, in *Proceedings of the 9th Extended Semantic Web Conference (ESWC2012)*, Heraklion, Greece, 27–31 May 2012. Springer LNCS, vol. 7295

R.V. Guha, *Contexts: A Formalization and Some Applications*, Ph.D. thesis, Stanford University, STAN-CS-91-1399-Thesis.guha, 1991

R.V. Guha, Introducing schema.org: Search engines come together for a richer web, *Google Official Blog* (2011)

R.V. Guha, R. McCool, E. Miller, Semantic search, in *Proceedings of the 12th International World Wide Web Conference (WWW2003)*, 20–24 May 2003 (ACM, Budapest)

R.V. Guha, D. Brickley, S. Macbeth, Schema.org: evolution of structured data on the web. Commun. ACM **59**(2), 44–51 (2016)

K. Gunaratna, S. Lalithsena, A.P. Sheth, Alignment and dataset identification of linked data in Semantic Web. Wiley Interdiscip. Rev. Data Min. Knowl. Discov. **4**(2), 139–151 (2014)

S. Gupta, G.E. Kaiser, D. Neistadt, P. Grimm, DOM-based content extraction of HTML documents, in *Proceedings of the 12th International World Wide Web Conference (WWW2003)*, 20–24 May 2003 (ACM, Budapest)

S. Gupta, P.A. Szekely, C.A. Knoblock, A. Goel, M. Taheriyan, M. Muslea, Karma: a system for mapping structured sources into the Semantic Web, in *Proceedings of the 9th Extended Semantic Web Conference (ESWC2012): Revised Selected Papers*, Crete, Greece, 27–31 May 2012. Springer LNCS, vol. 7540

S. Hakimov, C. Unger, S. Walter, P. Cimiano, Applying semantic parsing to question answering over linked data: addressing the lexical gap, in *Proceedings of the 20th International Conference on Applications of Natural Language to Information Systems (NLDB2015)*, Passau, Germany, 17–19 June 2015. Springer LNCS, vol. 9103

H. Halpin, P.J. Hayes, J.P. McCusker, D.L. McGuinness, H.S. Thompson, When owl:sameAs isn't the same: an analysis of identity in linked data, in *Proceedings of the 9th International Semantic Web Conference (ISWC2010)*, 7–11 November 2010 (Springer, Shanghai)

J.B. Hansen, A. Beveridge, R. Farmer, L. Gehrmann, A.J.G. Gray, S. Khutan, T. Robertson, J. Val, Validata: an online tool for testing RDF data conformance, in *Proceedings of the 8th International Conference on Semantic Web Applications and Tools for Life Sciences (SWAT4LS2015)*, CEUR Workshop Proceedings, vol. 1546, Cambridge, UK, 7–10 December 2015

S. Harris, A. Seaborne, E. Prud'hommeaux (eds.), *SPARQL 1.1 Query Language*, W3C Recommendation, 21 March 2013. https://www.w3.org/TR/sparql11-query/

A. Harth, A. Hogan, R. Delbru, J. Umbrich, S. O'Riain, S. Decker, SWSE: answers before links! in *Proceedings of the Semantic Web Challenge 2007 Co-Located with the 6th International Semantic Web Conference (ISWC2007) and the 2nd Asian Semantic Web Conference (ASWC2007), CEUR Workshop Proceedings*, vol. 295, Busan, Korea, 11–15 November 2007

P. Hayes, *The Logic of Frames, Readings in Artificial Intelligence* (Morgan Kaufmann, Los Altos, CA, 1981)

P. Hayes (ed.), *RDF semantics*, W3C recommendation, 10 February 2004. https://www.w3.org/TR/sparql11-query/

G.W.F. Hegel, *Science of Logic*, vol. I, Section 3, Chapter 1, A. The Specific Quantum (Translated by A.V. Miller). Atlantic Highlands: Humanities Paperback Library, Originally appeared (1812)

J. Hipp, U. Güntzer, G. Nakhaeizadeh, Algorithms for association rule mining—a general survey and comparison. ACM SIGKDD Explor. Newsl. **2**(1), 58–64 (2000)

R. Hoekstra, The knowledge reengineering bottleneck. Semant. Web J. **1**(1–2), 111–115 (2010)

J. Hoffart, F.M. Suchanek, K. Berberich, G. Weikum, YAGO2: a spatially and temporally enhanced knowledge base from Wikipedia. Artif. Intell. **194**, 28–61 (2013)

K. Höffner, S. Walter, E. Marx, R. Usbeck, J. Lehmann, A.N. Ngomo, Survey on challenges of question answering in the Semantic Web. Semant. Web J. **8**(6), 895–920 (2017)

A. Hogan, A. Harth, S. Decker, Performing object consolidation on the Semantic Web data graph, in *Proceedings of the 16th International World Wide Web Conference (WWW2007): Workshop I3: Identity, Identifiers, Identification, Entity-Centric Approaches to Information and Knowledge Management on the Web, CEUR Workshop Proceedings*, vol. 249, Banff, Canada, 8 May 2007

S.M. Inzalkar, J. Sharma, A survey on text mining-techniques and application. Int. J. Res. Sci. Eng. **14**, 1–14 (2015)

K. Janowicz, P. Hitzler, B. Adams, D. Kolas, C. Vardeman, Five stars of linked data vocabulary use. Semant. Web J. **5**(3), 173–176 (2014)

E. Kärle, U. Şimşek, D. Fensel, semantify.it, a platform for creation, publication and distribution of semantic annotations, in *Proceedings of the 11th International Conference on Advances in Semantic Processing (SEMAPRO2017)*, IARIA, Barcelona, Spain, 12–16 November 2017

E. Kärle, U. Şimşek, O. Panasiuk, D. Fensel, Building an ecosystem for the tyrolean tourism knowledge graph, in *Proceedings of the International Conference on Trends in Web Engineering (ICWE2018), International Workshops, MATWEP, EnWot, KD-Web, WEOD, TourismKG: Revised Selected Papers*, Caceres, Spain, 5 June 2018. Springer LNCS, vol. 11153

L. Karoui, M.-A. Aufaure, N. Bennacer, Ontology discovery from web pages: application to tourism, in *Proceedings of the Workshop on Knowledge Discovery and Ontologies (ECML/ PKDD2004)*, Pisa, Italy, 20–24 September 2004

M. Kejriwal, C. Knoblock, P. Szekely, Constructing domain-specific knowledge graphs, in *Proceedings of the 16th International Semantic Web Conference (ISWC2017): Tutorial*, Vienna, Austria, 21–25 October 2017. https://usc-isi-i2.github.io/ISWC17/

M. Kifer, G. Lausen, J. Wu, Logical foundations of object-oriented and frame-based languages. J. ACM **42**(4), 741–843 (May 1995)

J. Kim, C. Unger, A.N. Ngomo, A. Freitas, Y. Hahm, J. Kim, G. Choi, J. Kim, R. Usbeck, M. Kang, K. Choi, OKBQA: an open collaboration framework for development of natural language question-answering over knowledge bases, in *Proceedings of the 16th International Semantic Web Conference (ISWC 2017): Posters & Demonstrations and Industry Tracks, CEUR Workshop Proceedings*, vol. 1963, Vienna, Austria, 23–25 October 2017

J.M. Kleinberg, Authoritative sources in a hyperlinked environment. J. ACM **46**(5), 604–632 (1999)

T. Knap, J. Michelfeit, M. Necaský, Linked open data aggregation: conflict resolution and aggregate quality, in *Proceedings of the 36th Annual IEEE Computer Software and Applications Conference Workshops (COMP-SAC2012)*, IEEE Computer Society, Izmir, Turkey, 16–20 July 2012

H. Knublauch, D. Kontokostas (eds.), *Shapes Constraint Language (SHACL)*. W3C recommendation, 20 July 2017. https://www.w3.org/TR/shacl/

D. Kontokostas, P. Westphal, S. Auer, S. Hellmann, J. Lehmann, R. Cornelissen, A. Zaveri, Test-driven evaluation of linked data quality, in *Proceedings of the 23rd International Conference on World Wide Web (WWW2014)*, 07–11 April 2014 (ACM, Seoul)

J. Kopecký, T. Vitvar, C. Bournez, J. Farrell, SAWSDL: semantic annotations for WSDL and XML schema. IEEE Internet Comput. **11**(6), 60–67 (2007)

N. Korula, S. Lattanzi, An efficient reconciliation algorithm for social networks. Proc. Very Large Data Bases Endow. **7**(5), 377–388 (2014)

R. Kowalski, Predicate Logic as a Programming Language Memo 70, Department of Artificial Intelligence, Edinburgh University. Also in *Proceedings IFIP Congress*, (North Holland Publishing, Stockholm, 1974), pp. 569–574

S. Lalithsena, P. Hitzler, A.P. Sheth, P. Jain, Automatic domain identification for linked open data, in *Proceedings of the International Joint Conference on Web Intelligence (WI2013) and Intelligent Agent Technologies (IAT2013)*, IEEE Computer Society, Atlanta, 17–20 November 2013

D. Lange, C. Böhm, F. Naumann, Extracting structured information from Wikipedia articles to populate infoboxes, in *Proceedings of the 19th Conference on Information and Knowledge Management (CIKM2010)*, 26–30 October 2010 (ACM, Toronto)

A. Langegger, W. Wöß, Langegger: XLWrap–querying and integrating arbitrary spreadsheets with SPARQL, in *Proceedings of the 8th International Semantic Web Conference (ISWC 2009)*, 25–29 October 2009 (Springer, Chantilly, VA)

M. Lanthaler, C. Guetl, Hydra: a vocabulary for hypermedia-driven web APIs, in *Proceedings of the 22nd International World Wide Web Conference (WWW2013): Workshop on Linked Data on the Web (LDOW2013), CEUR Workshop Proceedings*, vol. 996, Rio de Janeiro, Brazil, 14 May 2013

J. Lehmann, R. Isele, M. Jakob, A. Jentzsch, D. Kontokostas, P.N. Mendes, S. Hellmann, M. Morsey, P. van Kleef, S. Auer, C. Bizer, DBpedia—a large-scale, multilingual knowledge base extracted from Wikipedia. Semant. Web J. **6**(2), 167–195 (2015)

D.B. Lenat, CYC: a large-scale investment in knowledge infrastructure. Commun. ACM **38**(11), 33–38 (1995)

D.B. Lenat, R.V. Guha, *Building Large Knowledge-Based Systems; Representation and Inference in the Cyc Project*, 1st edn. (Addison-Wesley Longman, Reading, MA, 1989)

P. Lertvittayakumjorn, N. Kertkeidkachorn, R. Ichise, Resolving range violations in DBpedia, in *Proceedings of the 7th Joint International Semantic Technology Conference (JIST2017)*, Gold Coast, Australia, 10–12 November 2017. Springer LNCS, vol. 10675

W. Li, C. Clifton, SEMINT: a tool for identifying attribute correspondences in heterogeneous databases using neural networks. Data Knowl. Eng. **33**(1), 49–84 (2000)

Y. Li, J. Gao, C. Meng, Q. Li, L. Su, B. Zhao, W. Fan, J. Han, A survey on truth discovery. ACM SIGKDD Explor. Newsl. **17**(2), 1–16 (2016)

J. Li, M. Zhou, G. Qi, N. Lao, T. Ruan, J. Du (eds.), *Knowledge Graph and Semantic Computing. Language, Knowledge, and Intelligence—Second China Conference (CCKS2017): Revised Selected Papers*, Chengdu, China, 26–29 August 2017. Springer CCIS, vol. 784

J. Liang, Y. Xiao, Y. Zhang, S. Hwang, H. Wang, Graph-based wrong IsA relation detection in a large-scale lexical taxonomy, in *Proceedings of the 31st Conference on Artificial Intelligence (AAAI2017)*, 4–9 February 2017 (AAAI Press, San Francisco)

L. Ma, Z. Su, Y. Pan, L. Zhang, T. Liu, RStar: an RDF storage and query system for enterprise resource management, in *Proceedings of the 13th International Conference on Information and knowledge Management (CIKM2004)*, 8–13 November 2004 (ACM, Washington)

Y. Ma, H. Gao, T. Wu, G. Qi, Learning disjointness axioms with association rule mining and its application to inconsistency detection of linked data, in *Proceedings of the 8th Chinese Semantic Web and Web Science Conference (CSWS2014): Revised Selected Papers*, Wuhan, China, 8–12 August 2014. Springer CCIS 480

R. Mahanti, *Data Quality: Dimensions, Measurement, Strategy, Management, and Governance* (ASQ Quality Press, Milwaukee, 2019)

F. Mahdisoltani, J. Biega, F.M. Suchanek, YAGO3: a knowledge base from multilingual Wikipedias, in *Proceedings of Seventh Biennial Conference on Innovative Data Systems Research (CIDR2015), Online Proceedings*, Asilomar, CA, 4–7 January 2015. www.cidrdb.org

S. Malyshev, M. Krötzsch, L. González, J. Gonsior, A. Bielefeldt, Getting the most out of Wikidata: semantic technology usage in Wikipedia's knowledge graph, in *Proceedings of 17th International Semantic Web Conference (ISWC 2018)*, Monterey, CA, 8–12 October 2018. Springer LNCS, vol. 11137

D.L. Martin, M. Paolucci, S.A. McIlraith, M.H. Burstein, D.V. McDermott, D.L. McGuinness, B. Parsia, T.R. Payne, M. Sabou, M. Solanki, N. Srinivasan, K.P. Sycara, Bringing semantics to web services: the OWL-S approach, in *Proceedings of the Semantic Web Services and Web Process Composition (SWSWPC2004): 1st International Workshop, Revised Selected Papers*, San Diego, 6 July 2004. Springer LNCS, vol. 3387

E. Marx, R. Usbeck, A.N. Ngomo, K. Höffner, J. Lehmann, S. Auer, Towards an open question answering architecture, in *Proceedings of the 10th International Conference on Semantic Systems (SEMANTICS2014)*, 4–5 September 2014 (ACM, Leipzig)

E. Marx, T. Soru, D. Esteves, A.N. Ngomo, J. Lehmann, An open question answering framework, in *Proceedings of the 14th International Semantic Web Conference (ISWC2015): Posters & Demonstrations Track, CEUR Workshop Proceedings*, vol. 1486, Bethlehem, 11 October 2015

M. McTear, Z. Callejas, D. Griol, *The Conversational Interface: Talking to Smart Devices* (Springer, Cham, 2016)

A. Melo, H. Paulheim, Detection of relation assertion errors in knowledge graphs, in *Proceedings of the 9th International Conference on Knowledge Capture (K-CAP2017)*, 4–6 December 2017 (ACM, Austin)

P.N. Mendes, H. Mühleisen, C. Bizer, Sieve: linked data quality assessment and fusion, in *Proceedings of the 2nd International Workshop on Linked Web Data Management (LWDM 2012), in Conjunction with the 15th International Conference on Extending Database Technology (EDBT2012): Workshops*, 30 March 2012 (ACM, Berlin)

D. Menestrina, S. Whang, H. Garcia-Molina, Evaluating entity resolution results. Proc. Very Large Data Bases Endow. **3**(1–2), 208–219 (2010)

P. Mika, On Schema.org and why it matters for the web. IEEE Internet Comput. **19**(4), 52–55 (2015)

D. Milward, M. Beveridge, Ontology-based dialogue systems, in *Proceedings of the 3rd International Joint Conference on Artificial Intelligence (IJCAI2013): Workshop on Knowledge and Reasoning in Practical Dialogue Systems*, Acapulco, Mexico, 10 August 2003

T.M. Mitchell, W.W. Cohen, E.R. Hruschka Jr., P.P. Talukdar, B. Yang, J. Betteridge, A. Carlson, B.D. Mishra, M. Gardner, B. Kisiel, J. Krishnamurthy, N. Lao, K. Mazaitis, T. Mohamed, N. Nakashole, E.A. Platanios, A. Ritter, M. Samadi, B. Settles, R.C. Wang, D. Wijaya, A. Gupta, X. Chen, A. Saparov, M. Greaves, J. Welling, Never-ending learning. Commun. ACM **61**(5), 103–115 (2018)

B. Mohit, Named entity recognition, in *Natural Language Processing of Semitic Languages*, ed. by I. Zitouni, (Springer, Berlin, 2014), pp. 221–245

A. Moschitti, K. Tymoshenko, P. Alexopoulos, A.D. Walker, M. Nicosia, G. Vetere, A. Faraotti, M. Monti, J.Z. Pan, H. Wu, Y. Zhao, Question answering and knowledge graphs, in *Exploiting Linked Data and Knowledge Graphs in Large Organisations*, ed. by J. Z. Pan, G. Vetere, J. M. Gómez-Pérez, H. Wu, (Springer, Cham, 2017)

E. Motta, J. Domingue, L. Cabral, M. Gaspari, IRS-II: a framework and infrastructure for Semantic Web services, in *Proceedings of the 2nd International Semantic Web Conference (ISWC 2003)*, Sanibel Island, 20–23 October 2003. Springer LNCS, vol. 2870

E. Muñoz, A. Hogan, A. Mileo, Triplifying Wikipedia's tables, in *Proceedings of the 1st International Workshop on Linked Data for Information Extraction (LD4IE2013) Co-Located with the 12th International Semantic Web Conference (ISWC2013), CEUR Workshop Proceeding*, vol. 1057, Sydney, Australia, 21 October 2013

A. Newell, The knowledge level. Artif. Intell. **18**(1), 87–127 (1982)

A.N. Ngomo, S. Auer, LIMES—a time-efficient approach for large-scale link discovery on the web of data, in *Proceedings of the 22nd International Joint Conference on Artificial Intelligence (IJ-CAI2011)*, 16–22 July 2011 (AAAI Press, Barcelona)

A. Nikolov, V.S. Uren, E. Motta, A.N.D. Roeck, Integration of semantically annotated data by the KnoFuss architecture, in *Proceedings of the 16th International Conference on Knowledge Engineering and Knowledge Management (EKAW2008): Practice and Patterns*, Acitrezza, Italy, 29 September–2 October 2008. Springer LNCS, vol. 5268

N. Noy, Y. Gao, A. Jain, A. Narayanan, A. Patterson, J. Taylor, Industry-scale knowledge graphs: lessons and challenges. ACM Queue **17**(2), 48–75 (2019)

A.G. Nuzzolese, A. Gangemi, V. Presutti, P. Ciancarini, Type inference through the analysis of Wikipedia links, in *Proceedings of the 21st International Conference on World Wide Web*

(WWW2012): *Workshop on Linked Data on the Web (LDOW2012), CEUR Workshop Proceedings*, vol. 937, Lyon, France, 16 April 2012

M.J. O'Connor, C. Halaschek-Wiener, M.A. Musen, Mapping master: a flexible approach for mapping spreadsheets to OWL, in *Proceedings of the 9th International Semantic Web Conference (ISWC2010): Revised Selected Papers*, Shanghai, China, 7–11 November 2010. Springer LNCS, vol. 6497

J.Z. Pan, D. Calvanese, T. Eiter, I. Horrocks, M. Kifer, F. Lin, Y. Zhao (eds.), *Reasoning Web: Logical Foundation of Knowledge Graph Construction and Query Answering—12th International Summer School 2016: Tutorial Lectures*, Aberdeen, UK, 5–9 September 2017a. Springer LNCS, vol. 9885

J. Z. Pan, G. Vetere, J. M. Gómez-Pérez, H. Wu (eds.), *Exploiting Linked Data and Knowledge Graphs in Large Organisations* (Springer, Cham, 2017b)

O. Panasiuk, E. Kärle, U. Şimşek, D. Fensel, Defining tourism domains for semantic annotation of web content, in *Proceedings of the Conference on Information and Communication Technologies in Tourism (ENTER2018): Research Notes*, Jönköping, Sweden, 24–26 January 2018a

O. Panasiuk, Z. Akbar, T. Gerrier, D. Fensel, Representing GeoData for tourism with Schema.org, in *Proceedings of the 4th International Conference on Geographical Information Systems Theory, Applications and Management (GISTAM2018)*, 17–19 March 2018b (SciTePress, Funchal, Portugal)

O. Panasiuk, Z. Akbar, U. Şimşek, D. Fensel, Enabling conversational tourism assistants through Schema.org mapping, in *Proceedings of the European Semantic Web Conference (ESWC2018): Satellite Event, Revised Selected Papers*, Hersonissos, Greece, 3–7 June 2018c. Springer LNCS, vol. 11155

O. Panasiuk, O. Holzknecht, U. Şimşek, E. Kärle, D. Fensel, Verification and validation of semantic annotations, in *Proceedings of the 12th A.P. Ershov Informatics Conference (PSI 2019)*, Novosibirsk, Russia, 2–5 July 2019 (Springer). Preprint. https://arxiv.org/abs/1904.01353

L. Papaleo, N. Pernelle, F. Saïs, C. Dumont, Logical detection of invalid SameAs statements in RDF data, in *Proceedings of the 19th International Conference on Knowledge Engineering and Knowledge Management (EKAW2014)*, Linköping, Sweden, 24–28 November 2014. Springer LNCS, vol. 8876

P. Paritosh, The missing science of knowledge curation: improving incentives for large-scale knowledge curation, in *Proceedings of the International World Wide Web Conference (WWW2018)*, 23–27 April 2018 (ACM, Lyon)

P.F. Patel-Schneider, Analyzing Schema.org, in *Proceedings of the 13th International Semantic Web Conference (ISWC2014)*, Riva del Garda, Italy, 19–23 October 2014. Springer LNCS, vol. 8796

P.F. Patel-Schneider, I. Horrocks, Position paper: a comparison of two modelling paradigms in the Semantic Web, in *Proceedings of the 15th International World Wide Web Conference (WWW2006)*, 23–26 May 2006 (ACM, Edinburgh)

A.A. Patil, S.A. Oundhakar, A.P. Sheth, K. Verma, METEOR-S web service annotation framework, in *Proceedings of the 13th International Conference on World Wide Web (WWW2004)*, 17–20 May 2004 (ACM, New York)

H. Paulheim, Identifying wrong links between datasets by multi-dimensional outlier detection, in *Proceedings of the 3rd International Workshop on Debugging Ontologies and Ontology Mappings (WoDOOM2014) Co-Located with the 11th Extended Semantic Web Conference (ESWC2014), CEUR Workshop Proceedings*, vol. 1162, Hersonissou, Greece, 26 May 2014

H. Paulheim, Knowledge graph refinement: a survey of approaches and evaluation methods. Semant. Web J. **8**(3), 489–508 (2017)

H. Paulheim, Machine learning with and for Semantic Web knowledge graphs, ed. by C. d'Amato, M. Theobald, in *Proceedings of the 14th International Summer School 2018: Reasoning Web. Learning, Uncertainty, Streaming, and Scalability: Tutorial Lectures*, Esch-sur-Alzette, Luxembourg, 22–26 September 2018a. Springer LNCS, vol. 11078

H. Paulheim, How much is a triple? Estimating the cost of knowledge graph creation, in *Proceedings of the 17th International Semantic Web Conference (ISWC2018): Posters & Demonstrations, Industry and Blue Sky Ideas Tracks, CEUR Workshop Proceedings*, vol. 2180, Monterey, 8–12 October 2018b

H. Paulheim, C. Bizer, Type inference on noisy RDF data, in *Proceedings of the 12th International Semantic Web Conference (ISWC2013)*, Sydney, Australia, 21–25 October 2013. Springer LNCS, vol. 8218

H. Paulheim, C. Bizer, Improving the quality of linked data using statistical distributions. Int. J. Semant. Web Inf. Syst. **10**(2), 63–86 (2014)

H. Paulheim, M. Sabou, M. Cochez, W. Beek, Evaluation of knowledge graphs, ed. by P.A. Bonatti, S. Decker, A. Polleres, V. Presutti, in *Knowledge Graphs: New Directions for Knowledge Representation on the Semantic Web (Dagstuhl Seminar 18371)*, Dagstuhl Rep. **8**(9), 29–111 (2019)

N. Pernelle, J. Raad, F. Saïs, Detection of invalid identity links statements in RDF knowledge graphs. Presented in the 21st International Conference on Knowledge Engineering and Knowledge Management (EKAW2018): Workshops: Symbolic methods for data-interlinking, Nancy, France, 12–16 November 2018. https://project.inria.fr/ekaw2018/workshops/

L. Pipino, Y.W. Lee, R.Y. Wang, Data quality assessment. Commun. ACM **45**(4), 211–218 (2002)

J. Plu, G. Rizzo, R. Troncy, ADEL: ADaptable Entity Linking: a hybrid approach to link entities with linked data for information extraction. Semant. Web J. (Special Issue on Linked Data for Information Extraction) **1**, 1–5 (2017)

G. Qi, J. Tang, J. Du, J.Z. Pan, Y. Yu (eds.), *Linked Data and Knowledge Graph—7th Chinese Semantic Web Symposium and 2nd Chinese Web Science Conference (CSWS2013): Revised Selected Papers*, Shanghai, China, 12–16 August 2013. Springer CCIS, vol. 406

G. Qi, H. Chen, K. Liu, H. Wang, Q. Ji, T. Wu, *Knowledge Graph* (Springer, Cham, 2020)

J. Raad, N. Pernelle, F. Saïs, Detection of contextual identity links in a knowledge base, in *Proceedings of the Knowledge Capture Conference (K-CAP2017)*, 4–6 December 2017 (ACM, Austin)

J. Raad, W. Beek, F. van Harmelen, N. Pernelle, F. Saïs, Detecting erroneous identity links on the web using network metrics, in *Proceeding of the 17th International Semantic Web Conference (ISWC2018)*, Monterrey, 8–12 October 2018. Springer LNCS, vol. 111

Y. Raimond, C. Sutton, M.B. Sandler, Automatic interlinking of music datasets on the Semantic Web, in *Proceedings of the 17th International World Wide Web Conference (WWW2008): Workshop on Linked Data on the Web (LDOW2008), CEUR Workshop Proceedings*, vol. 369, Beijing, China, 22 April 2008

R. Ramakrishnan, J.D. Ullman, A survey of deductive database systems. J. Log. Program. **23**(2), 125–149 (1995)

S.K. Reed, A. Pease, Reasoning from imperfect knowledge. Cogn. Syst. Res. **41**, 56–72 (2017)

W. Reisig, *Understanding Petri Nets—Modeling Techniques, Analysis Methods, Case Studies* (Springer, Cham, 2013)

T. Rekatsinas, X. Chu, I.F. Ilyas, C. Ré, HoloClean: holistic data repairs with probabilistic inference. Proc. Very Large Data Bases Endow. **10**(11), 1190–1201 (2017)

D. Roman, J. de Bruijn, A. Mocan, H. Lausen, J. Domingue, C. Bussler, D. Fensel, WWW: WSMO, WSML, and WSMX in a nutshell, in *Proceedings of the 1st Asian Semantic Web Conference (ASWC2006)*, Beijing, China, 3–7 September 2006. Springer LNCS, vol. 4185

D. Roman, J. Kopecký, T. Vitvar, J. Domingue, D. Fensel, WSMO-Lite and hRESTS: lightweight semantic annotations for web services and RESTful APIs. J. Web Semant. **31**, 39–58 (2015)

M. Rubiolo, M.L. Caliusco, G. Stegmayer, M. Gareli, M. Coronel, Knowledge source discovery: an experience using ontologies, WordNet and artificial neural networks, in *Proceedings of the 13th International Conference on Knowledge-Based and Intelligent Information and Engineering Systems (KES2009)*, Santiago, Chile, 28–30 September 2009. Springer LNCS, vol. 5712

A. Rula, M. Palmonari, S. Rubinacci, A.N. Ngomo, J. Lehmann, A. Maurino, D. Esteves, TISCO: temporal scoping of facts. J. Web Semant. **54**, 72–86 (2019)

A.T. Schreiber, B. Wielinga, J. Breuker, *KADS: A Principled Approach to Knowledge-Based System Development, Knowledge-Based Systems*, vol 11 (Academic, London, 1993)

A.T. Schreiber, G. Schreiber, H. Akkermans, A. Anjewierden, N. Shadbolt, R. de Hoog, W. Van de Velde, N.R. Shadbolt, B. Wielinga, *Knowledge Engineering and Management: The CommonKADS Methodolog* (MIT Press, Cambridge, MA, 2000)

A. Schultz, A. Matteini, R. Isele, P.N. Mendes, C. Bizer, C. Becker, LDIF—a framework for large-scale linked data integration, in *Proceedings of the 21st International World Wide Web Conference (WWW2012): Developers Track*, Lyon, France, 18–20 April 2012

S. Shehata, F. Karray, M.S. Kamel, An efficient concept-based mining model for enhancing text clustering. IEEE Trans. Knowl. Data Eng. **22**(10), 1360–1371 (2010)

H.A. Simon, *Models of Man: Social and Rational-Mathematical Essays on Rational Human Behavior in a Social Setting* (Wiley, New York, 1957)

U. Şimşek, D. Fensel, Intent generation for goal-oriented dialogue systems based on Schema.org annotations. Presented in the 1st International Workshop on Chatbots Co-Located with the 12th International Conference on Web and Social Media (ICWSM2018), Stanford, 25–28 June 2018a. http://datainnovation.soic.indiana.edu:8080/chatbot/index.html

U. Şimşek, D. Fensel, Now we are talking! Flexible and open goal-oriented dialogue systems for accessing touristic services, in *Proceedings of the Conference on Information and Communication Technologies in Tourism (ENTER2018): Research Notes*, Jönköping, Sweden, 24--26 January 2018b

U. Şimşek, E. Kärle, O. Holzknecht, D. Fensel, Domain specific semantic validation of schema.org annotations, in *Proceedings of the 11th International A. P. Ershov Informatics Conference (PSI 2017)*, Moscow, Russia, 27–29 June 2017. Springer LNCS, vol. 10742 (2018a)

U. Şimşek, E. Kärle, D. Fensel, Machine readable web APIs with Schema.org action annotations, in *Proceedings of the 14th International Conference on Semantic Systems (SEMANTICS 2018)*, 10–13 September 2018b (Elsevier, Vienna)

U. Şimşek, E. Kärle, D. Fensel, RocketRML—a NodeJS implementation of a use-case specific RML mapper, in *Proceedings of 1st Knowledge Graph Building Workshop Co-Located with the 16th Extended Semantic Web Conference (ESWC2019), CEUR Workshop Proceedings*, Portoroz, Slovenia, 3 June 2019a

U. Şimşek, K. Angele, E. Kärle, O. Panasiuk, D. Fensel, A formal approach for customization of schema.org based on SHACL, Technical Report (2019b). https://arxiv.org/abs/1906.06492

K. Singh, A.S. Radhakrishna, A. Both, S. Shekarpour, I. Lytra, R. Usbeck, A. Vyas, A. Khikmatullaev, D. Punjani, C. Lange, M.E. Vidal, J. Lehmann, S. Auer, Why reinvent the wheel: let's build question answering systems together, in *Proceedings of the 2018 International World Wide Web Conference (WWW2018)*, Lyon, France, 23–27 April 2018

J. Sleeman, T. Finin, Type prediction for efficient coreference resolution in heterogeneous semantic graphs, in *Proceedings of the 7th International Conference on Semantic Computing (ICSC2013)*, IEEE Computer Society, Irvine, 16–18 September 2013

J. Sleeman, T. Finin, A. Joshi, Topic modeling for RDF graphs, in *Proceedings of the 3rd International Workshop on Linked Data for Information Extraction (LD4IE2015) Co-Located with the 14th International Semantic Web Conference (ISWC2015), CEUR Workshop Proceedings*, vol. 1467, Bethlehem, 12 October 2015

R. Socher, D. Chen, C.D. Manning, A.Y. Ng, Reasoning with neural tensor networks for knowledge base completion, in *Proceedings of the 26th International Conference on Neural Information Processing Systems (NIPS2013)—Volume 1*, Lake Tahoe, 05–10 December 2013

D. Sonntag, R. Engel, G. Herzog, A. Pfalzgraf, N. Pfleger, M. Romanelli, N. Reithinger, SmartWeb handheld—multimodal interaction with ontological knowledge bases and Semantic Web services. Artif. Intell. Hum. Comput., 272–295 (2007)

J.F. Sowa, Semantic networks, in *Encyclopedia of Artificial Intelligence*, ed. by S. C. Shapiro, 2nd edn., (Wiley, New York, 1992). http://www.jfsowa.com/pubs/semnet.pdf

M. Sporny, D. Longley, G. Kellogg, M. Lanthaler, N. Lindström (eds.), *JSON-LD 1.0*. W3C recommendation, 16 January 2014. https://www.w3.org/TR/json-ld/

S. Staab, R. Studer, *Ontology Handbook* (Springer, Berlin, 2010)

F. Stegmaier, U. Gröbner, M. Döller, H. Kosch, G. Baese, Evaluation of current RDF database solutions, in *Proceedings of the 10th International Workshop on Semantic Multimedia Database Technologies (SeMuDaTe2009) in Conjunction with the 4th International Conference on Semantics and Digital Media Technologies (SAMT2009), CEUR Workshop Proceedings*, vol. 539, Graz, Austria, 2 December 2009

G. Stegmayer, M.L. Caliusco, O. Chiotti, M.R. Galli, ANN-agent for distributed knowledge source discovery, in *Proceedings of the on the Move to Meaningful Internet Systems (OTM2007): Confederated International Workshops and Posters, AWeSOMe, CAMS, OTM Academy Doctoral Consortium, MONET, OnToContent, ORM, PerSys, PPN, RDDS, SSWS, and SWWS 2007*, Vilamoura, Portugal, 25–30 November 2007. Springer LNCS, vol. 4805

R.J. Sternberg, K. Sternberg, *Cognitive Psychology*, 6th edn. (Wadsworth, Cengage Learning, Belmont, CA, 2009)

A. Stolz, M. Hepp, Integrating product classification standards into Schema.org: eCl@ss and UNSPSC on the web of data, in *Proceedings of on the Move to Meaningful Internet Systems. OTM 2017 Workshops*, Rhodes, Greece, 23–28 October 2017 (2018). Springer LNCS, vol. 10697

R. Studer, V.R. Benjamins, D. Fensel, Knowledge engineering: principles and methods. Data Knowl. Eng. **25**(1–2), 161–197 (1998)

F.M. Suchanek, G. Kasneci, G. Weikum, Yago: a core of semantic knowledge, in *Proceedings of the 16th International World Wide Web Conference (WWW2007)*, 8–12 May 2007 (ACM, Banff, Canada)

G. Töpper, M. Knuth, H. Sack, DBpedia ontology enrichment for inconsistency detection, in *Proceedings of the 8th International Conference on Semantic Systems (SEMANTICS2012)*, 5–7 September 2012 (ACM, Graz)

V. Uren, P. Cimiano, J. Iria, S. Handschuh, M. Vargas-Vera, E. Motta, F. Ciravegna, Semantic annotation for knowledge management: requirements and a survey of the state of the art. Web Semant. Sci. Serv. Agents World Wide Web Arch. **4**(1), 14–28 (2006)

D. Van Deursen, C. Poppe, G. Martens, E. Mannens, R. Van de Walle, XML to RDF conversion: a generic approach, in *Proceedings of the 4th International Conference on Automated solutions for Cross Media Content and Multi-Channel Distribution (AXMEDIS2008)*, 17–19 November 2008 (IEEE, Florence)

M. Van Erp, S. Hellmann, J.P. McCrae, C. Chiarcos, K. Choi, J. Gracia, Y. Hayashi, S. Koide, P.N. Mendes, H. Paulheim, H. Takeda (eds.), Knowledge graphs and language technology, in *Proceedings of the 15th International Semantic Web Conference (ISWC2016): International Workshops: KEKI and NLP&DBpedia*, Kobe, Japan, 17–21 October 2016. Revised selected papers. Springer LNCS, vol. 10579 (2017)

M.Y. Vardi, How the hippies destroyed the Internet. Commun. ACM **61**(7), 9 (2018)

R. Verborgh, T. Steiner, D.V. Deursen, J.D. Roo, R.V. de Walle, J.G. Vallés, Capturing the functionality of web services with functional descriptions. Multimed. Tools Appl. **64**(2), 365–387 (2013)

R. Verborgh, A. Harth, M. Maleshkova, S. Stadtmüller, T. Steiner, M. Taheriyan, R. Van de Walle, Survey of semantic description of REST APIs, in *REST: Advanced Research Topics and Practical Applications*, ed. by C. Pautasso, E. Wilde, R. Alarcon, (Springer, Berlin, 2014), pp. 69–89

S. Vijayarani, M.J. Ilamathi, M. Nithya, Preprocessing techniques for text mining-an overview. Int. J. Comput. Sci. Commun. Netw. **5**(1), 7–16 (2015)

B. Villazón-Terrazas, N. García-Santa, Y. Ren, A. Faraotti, H. Wu, Y. Zhao, G. Vetere, J.Z. Pan, Knowledge graph foundations, in *Exploiting Linked Data and Knowledge Graphs in Large Organisations*, ed. by J. Z. Pan, G. Vetere, J. M. Gómez-Pérez, H. Wu, (Springer, Cham, 2017)

J. Volz, C. Bizer, M. Gaedke, G. Kobilarov, Discovering and maintaining links on the web of data, in *Proceedings of the 8th International Semantic Web Conference (ISWC2009)*, Chantilly, 25–29 October 2009. Springer LNCS, vol. 5823

D. Vrandečić, M. Krötzsch, Wikidata: a free collaborative knowledge base. Commun. ACM **57**(10), 78–85 (2014)

R.Y. Wang, A product perspective on total data quality management. Commun. ACM **41**(2), 58–65 (1998)

R.Y. Wang, D.M. Strong, Beyond accuracy: what data quality means to data consumers. J. Manag. Inf. Syst. **12**(4), 5–33 (1996)

R.Y. Wang, M. Ziad, Y.W. Lee, *Data Quality* (Kluwer Academic Publisher, Norwell, MA, 2001)

R. West, E. Gabrilovich, K. Murphy, S. Sun, R. Gupta, D. Lin, Knowledge base completion via search-based question answering, in *Proceedings of the 23rd International World Wide Web Conference (WWW2014)*, 07–11 April 2014 (ACM, Seoul)

D. Wienand, H. Paulheim, Detecting incorrect numerical data in DBpedia, in *Proceedings of the 11th International European Semantic Web Conference (ESWC2014)*, Anissaras, Greece, 25–29 May 2014. Springer LNCS, vol. 8465

M.D. Wilkinson, M. Dumontier, I.J. Aalbersberg, G. Appleton, M. Axton, A. Baak, N. Blomberg, J.-W. Boiten, L.B. da Silva Santos, P.E. Bourne, J. Bouwman, A.J. Brookes, T. Clark, M. Crosas, I. Dillo, O. Dumon, S. Edmunds, C.T. Evelo, R. Finkers, A. Gonzalez-Beltran, A.J. Gray, P. Groth, C. Goble, J.S. Grethe, J. Heringa, P.A. 't Hoen, R. Hooft, T. Kuhn, R. Kok, J. Kok, S.J. Lusher, M.E. Martone, A. Mons, A.L. Packer, B. Persson, P. Rocca-Serra, M. Roos, R. van Schaik, S.-A. Sansone, E. Schultes, T. Sen-gstag, T. Slater, G. Strawn, M.A. Swertz, M. Thompson, J. van der Lei, E. van Mulligen, J. Velterop, A. Waagmeester, P. Wittenburg, K. Wolsten-croft, J. Zhao, B. Mons, The FAIR guiding principles for scientific data management and stewardship. Sci. Data **3**, 160018 (2016)

W.E. Winkler, *Overview of Record Linkage and Current Research Directions*. Research report series: Statistics #2006-2, Bureau of the Census (2006). https://www.census.gov/srd/papers/pdf/rrs2006-02.pdf

World Travel & Tourism Council, *Travel & Tourism Economic Impact 2018 World* (2018). https://www.wttc.org/-/media/files/reports/economic-impact-research/regions-2018/world2018.pdf

M. Wu, A. Marian, Corroborating answers from multiple web sources, in *Proceedings of the 10th International Workshop on the Web and Databases (WebDB2007)*, Beijing, China, 15 June 2007

H. Zafar, G. Napolitano, J. Lehmann, Formal query generation for question answering over knowledge bases, in *Proceedings of the 15th European Semantic Web Conference (ESWC2018)*, Hersonissos, Crete, 3–7 June 2018. Springer LNCS, vol. 10843

A. Zaveri, D. Kontokostas, M.A. Sherif, L. Bühmann, M. Morsey, S. Auer, J. Lehmann, User-driven quality evaluation of DBpedia, in *Proceedings of the 9th International Conference on Semantic Systems (I-SEMANTICS2013)*, 4–6 September 2013 (ACM, Graz)

A. Zaveri, A. Rula, A. Maurino, R. Pietrobon, J. Lehmann, S. Auer, Quality assessment for linked data: a survey. Semant. Web J. **7**(1), 63–93 (2016)

A. Zaveri, S. Dastgheib, C. Wu, T. Whetzel, R. Verborgh, P. Avillach, G. Korodi, R. Terryn, K.M. Jagodnik, P. Assis, M. Dumontier, smartAPI: towards a more intelligent network of web APIs, in *Proceedings of the 14th European Semantic Web Conference (ESWC2017)*, Portoroz, Slovenia, 28 May–1 June 2017. Springer LNCS, vol. 10250

Index

Printed in the United States
By Bookmasters